I0169910

WHERE YOU BEEN BOY

A LOVE STORY

BY

ROD MAGNER

Copyright © 2015 by Rod Magner

All rights reserved, including the right to reproduce this work in any form whatsoever, without permission in writing from the author, except for brief passages in connection with a review.

Cover design © by Rod Magner
Cover images © by Rod Magner, Sandy Kenyon

ISBN 978-0-9961572-1-6

Visit my business at magicair.com

or at littlemagic.com

Be sure to use the Glossary for technical terms.

CONTENTS

Zuni rockets fired at flotsam on the ocean

(Can't land aboard the carrier with them. They will careen out of their pods)

YELLOW STICKY NOTE: 3/2015

Once voted the first best line of a novel was this: "Frightened in the night, he reached for a match to light a candle. It was handed to him." It is the quality of the morning light, when my eyes first blink open, that begins each day the next chapter of my life. The "match" has been handed to me, by a Universe waiting to see whether I still believe I am master of my own destiny, dreams in the dark of night notwithstanding.

The manuscript for this book was passed around among a few friends exactly as you will read it here, in 1984. For the next thirty years it huddled silently in its dark green three ring binder, musty, in the basement file cabinet. As you read, simply follow along with the dates of each section. A single combat mission, July 1, 1970 is the focus and it reappears, as it did for me, like a ghost through the years. Fly with me on this and it'll all make sense. And remember to LOVE the morning Light.

PROLOGUE 1984

I looked at a close up photograph of an A4 Skyhawk recently and felt the old tingle of excitement that came from strapping on that tiny airplane and draping my arms over the cockpit sides, rolling down the long taxiways at Lemoore Naval Air Station, preparing for a low level "sandblower" flight across northern California into Oregon and into1 the test ranges of Fallon, Nevada. I looked at the crowded cockpit and remembered the first time I sat in one, thinking to myself that this was the kind of airplane I was supposed to fly into combat. Before that all the airplanes had been trainers and their character was lacking the hardware and cold bare bones feel the Skyhawk had. I sat alone in the massive hangar studying the knobs and dials and closed my eyes to see if I could reach for a handle, or point to an instrument quickly. I began the process of loving an airplane. We were touching, silently, in quiet whispers to each other. Six months of courtship lay ahead, six months of hard flying, practice bombing, night reconnaissance and finally more carrier qualifications with my first night carrier landings.

It has been sixteen years since that May day of 1968 I first met the Skyhawk. It seems like yesterday and I believe it always will. The combat has come and gone, the sand I kicked up on Nevada deserts long since found its resting place. No one, not a single person then, told me what it would be like sixteen years later. We were busy with a love affair and a mission we talked about in dive angles and fuze settings. We never spoke in pilots meeting about the future except in terms of careers and new weapons systems coming on line. The future of the world was being decided in different quarters. Some foggy distant voice of command that knew more than we did about everything gave us our orders. And we flew, flew because it was so incredibly exciting and hard and brave and made us feel like we had the world by the balls. Carrier pilots and big bombs and down on the deck at 500 knots. And what did you do today for excitement, poor wretched ordinary man? A wife and kids and TV and big business deal behind a desk? Some future that would be. I'm twenty-four and you can't tell me what I'm doing is not the best the world has to offer. This country has a war and she needs us. Needs us to pinpoint enemy targets and blast them from the face of the earth.

So I went to Vietnam and started bombing those targets. This is the story of one of those missions and how it came to haunt my life. I believe it is no coincidence that of all the combat I flew, just two personal cassette tapes were made on those missions. One of those, February 1, 1970, is here literally verbatim. Listening now to the voice of Lt. Magner in the quiet of my study is sobering. Like so many I was not prepared for the memory I was creating.

This is also a story of friends, of family, and of discovery. And learning the meaning of LOVE.

AND THEN WHEN I KILLED WITH MY WEAPONS

"You know," I said, "I tried to write a little piece about the war. But I got bogged down in structure. I wanted to write a story that I had never been told or read. War stories were driven by the writer's intimate passion to draw the reader into his gut wrenching experiences. But usually I think writers want more than anything to relive the war. Even if the words didn't say so, even if they tried to tell me how terrible killing was, behind it all was a message that at least he enjoyed being able to write about it. I wanted something different."

"And what was the result?" he asked, his eyes peering directly into mine. Friendly eyes really, but concerned for me. I saw them behind his glasses, big horn rimmed things that he had worn ever since I could remember.

"It is a minor disaster. I wrote a book only for me. One that could be read only by close friends like you. It's not so horrible really. I've let some friends read it. Their suggestions were measured and accurate, I expected that. I sat around for months and didn't touch the thing. Just thought about it. I was disappointed in myself. I decided it was a beautiful thing. Shiny and new. But it wasn't finished. The last chapter left more questions than it answered."

"Mags, I've always enjoyed your writing. It's been mostly letters. Christmas letters I guess, written in a stream of consciousness. But you were saying something. It can't be that bad can it?"

I was listening to Jim, one ear to him, the other to the voice of optimism inside of me. I was questioning why I thought I needed to write it in the first place. Years before, the motivation had been different that it was I when I finally sat down at the typewriter to formally begin it. Now, ten years had elapsed and my kids were growing up and life was a hell of a lot different than I imagined it was going to be. Screwing up financially, at the same time I was moving spiritually further than I would ever have dreamed.

"Jim," I said, drawing a deep breath, "you think you know where I've been. But you don't. No one does. And you have no idea how far I've come. Flying a jet off an aircraft carrier and dropping five hundred pound bombs on people half way around the world, that's a place you haven't been. That was the place I wanted to take people. I wanted them to see the pipper in my gunsight, pink against the green hillsides. I wanted to let them see the target, people running along a road and into the forest to escape my bombs. I wanted to get inside the bomb and explode with it. I wanted to know what it was like to be blown to bits, just so that I could FEEL, really understand, what the hell it was I was doing. How do you do that, Jim? How the hell do you tell people it was a miserable thing to be doing?" Frustration smothered me.

He blanched. "Well, I, ah, I guess you..."

I cut him short. My best friend, once dying of cancer. Michigan. Harvard. Years of friendship slipping around us now like a warm, soft blanket. "You gotta do it with words and the words gotta be right and what I wrote wasn't right. It didn't flow, you know. Didn't always make sense. Piss poor structure. But I wanted my words to speak the truth, to lay open the heart of that friggin war for me. I wanted my kids to read it and stop dead in their tracks when somebody asked them to smash the life out of a people they had never met. And I didn't want my story to sound like another glorious combat flight with philosophic moral reflections glued to the end of it."

"So you tried to write a story and it got confusing and you got lost in your adjectives and the message had all the life of words finger written on a steamy mirror. Now you're upset because you found out there's more to writing than being honest." Jim cocked his head to one side and with a sigh cracked a brotherly smile. I looked at him without speaking for a long moment. The years have been so good to us. Spared us. War had delivered me back to life. Hodgkin's disease had played with him beginning just after he graduated from Michigan with high honors. He beat it into remission. Twice now he'd done that. He was tough, sharp. He cut through bullshit to the heart of a matter with more candor than anyone I knew. I wanted him to read my manuscript, but had waited, mostly out of fear I suppose.

"I never read war novels now," I said. "I did when I was a kid and wanted to learn to fly. I hunted flying stories out. Everything I could get my hands on. After college I got my wish. I flew a jet, my own jet. Like the ads for the Navy promised."

Got to fly an attack jet, loaded with big 500 pound bombs. Got pretty good at it. At least I could land the sonofabitch. But that doesn't count anymore. What hurts is what I did with those bombs. What counts now is what I do with words. What counts now is what I say to my kids.

"That's why I'm pissed off. I wanted to write the story for them. But a story is supposed to have tension in it. Be full of energy and drama. You have to offer the reader a slice of your life that carries the aura of uncommon experience."

"Shit! "

"All I was offering was the death of fifteen members of an enemy road crew and my fucking innocence. A little gossamer border I crossed politely on February 1, 1970 about 10,000 feet over Vietnam. No big goddamn deal. Just talk about it. Look hard at it. That's what I thought."

"But what's deep down real important in my life isn't gonna be squat to somebody else unless I dress it up. Pack in characters and dialogue and tantalize the reader. Make him follow me down the dive, drag him with me through the mud of those days flying combat and the mind numbing boredom of being at sea. But that's what a book is. Make—believe."

Jim sat facing me, his hand pulling slowly at his chin. I took a breath through my nostrils, followed by a loud exhaling of the poisons my words had backed up in the lungs.

"So," he began, "what you have is a manuscript, not a book, a lot of pages, not a story, and you are mad at the world because it doesn't understand what YOU call honesty. Is that a fair assessment of where you are with it? "I shook my head and rubbed my right eye. It always helped to rub that eye when I was trapped by the Truth. I looked across the table at him and saw my dream of a book, cover and all, flash past his face. It was a fleeting image and it tumbled as it disappeared.

"Jim, I don't know that a book is important any more. Name one that stopped a war. Every word of wisdom ever written didn't come close to stopping me, who loved to fly more than anything else, from trading ambition for the lives of other human beings. Maybe there's time for figuring it all out when the war is over! That's what I thought. Suddenly, one day, you find you're in the real thing, a war that doesn't care what the hell you think of it."

"Mags," he said, his hands lifting up to express a kind of exasperation, "everybody already knows war is the shits. They don't need another book to tell them that. Stories that remind us how grotesque it is only numb us to it. What we need are stories that remind us of our humanity, not our inhumanity. If there were never another book written on war, there would be enough for anyone to learn everything they needed to know about them. But there are never enough stories that remind us how precious we are, how we are a part of everything that is, that ever was, or ever will be. That's what your story should be about."

"Jim, that's all I wanted to say." I wanted to scream it. I wanted my words to write a LOVE story. You know, the kid that spent hours in high school discussing with his Pastor the meaning of life. That loved life and wanted to live it gloriously. Life would be perfect for those who saw it that way." I wrote how I was almost killed in a car wreck when I was sixteen and this young nurse, a nun, talked to me. And she was the very essence of LOVE wrapping me in Light, but I didn't recognize it then. I looked at life in Mississippi; careened through Sierra canyons in my Skyhawk, loving — loving — loving everything I did.

And then, when I killed with my weapons, I hid it behind smug intellect and reason. But I couldn't hide it from my heart. Marriage came and two sons. I wrote about all of it. I wrote the pages and dated them and they flowed across the paper like oil poured on hot metal. I was loving the words and the feeling and releasing my guilt and learning more about something. But I couldn't finish it. It just flat ass stopped.

Jim nodded his head slowly. "You were discovering the next dimension of LOVE, correct?"

"I suppose," I muttered. "Most days it seems I have forgotten it all."

"But you want to teach about LOVE with your words don't you?...Teach it to the kids so they will change the world from one of war to peace." Jim spoke softly, the words drifting off to settle like dust on the furniture.

I felt a glow inside me rising. The sun that rose and set upon ideas in my mind was breaking the darkness of my anger with penetrating light. Internal Sunrises were private moments that only my eyes could reveal to an onlooker. Jim was reading them perfectly. "Yes, I wanted a LOVE story, one that told how I betrayed my inner light without ever understanding why. That told how I needed to admit I had done that, and which events in my life would restore me if I ex-

amined them. I should have called it a LOVE story from the beginning. But I garbaged it up with flying stories and literary devices to weave my message in. Every word was true, for me. In the end, though, it quit; my ego was being massaged even more than the truth.
"

"Is the book fun for you to read?" he asked.

"Oh, hell yes. I love it."

"Does it say what you want it to say?"

I stared at him before I could answer. I knew he meant did I say what I wanted to about LOVE.

"No. I want it to say more. Say more about LOVE. Sometimes I want to write it out like a school kid sent up to the blackboard when his teacher punishes him. LOVE LOVE LOVE, splattered across the entire page, on every page of the book; next to every page number, across the binding But then I suppose it would be overkill."

"You can't kill LOVE," he said. "Not the kind you're talking about."

Jim was a beautiful person. Demanding sometimes, gruff now and then, with little patience for short sighted, greedy people. His own struggles had taught him about LOVE, the kind that could end war. He seemed to straddle the realm of the spiritual and the concrete with ease. He had one foot in each. It was time to hand over to him what I had written. To face the cutting edge of his wisdom.

"Jim, here's the manuscript. First draft. See where it works and where it doesn't. There's 40,000 words there. Stashed in them is a combat cruise, a trail of events that followed, some streams of consciousness you like so much. It's dated, like a diary."

I handed the manilla folder with the typewritten pages in it across the table to him. "Do this. Return the chapters you think are worth keeping. Scratch all over them if you want."

"Alright," he said with a grin like a Cheshire cat, "I'll get a dozen red pencils, a good scissors, and find the 'love story' you buried in it somewhere."

I laughed and cracked another peanut open. We had shared peanuts and coke on our night discussions for years. If I brought the Coke, he brought the peanuts. It was a thing that had started back in college with talks that covered all the heavy issues we figured we could resolve then. World problems like women and nuclear war. We'd sit on the caved in leather couches in the Senior Study upstairs in the fraternity house, and talk till dawn. We didn't know hours then. We didn't know a lot, now that I look back, but we thought we did and that was the important thing.

I gave Jim the manuscript and we agreed to discuss it later. He would send me the chapters. Then, if our work schedules could be coordinated, we would fly in his Bonanza up to his father-in-law's lodge in northern Michigan, taking his daughter Katie and my son Scott. And a bag of peanuts.

Jim mailed the chapters back to me about a month later. There were not many in the envelope. And those were heavily marked. I was not surprised. I flipped through them forlornly, looking for the thread that tied them together in his mind. His margin remarks were brief, some critical, others applauding.

I had already decided that my manuscript was not a book. Or that it was even important. The process of writing it had been what was necessary for me. The dream of it becoming a book, important at first, now seemed less so. I was not sure why it did not matter. When a dream is so powerful at some point in my life, why does it fade so as I get older? Flying had been the all encompassing passion from my earliest years. Perhaps it was what I had done with that dream that discouraged me. Yet, somehow, the dream of a story for my boys could not be completely soured by that same process of reality.

"Dear Mags," he had written on a note, "Your LOVE story is here, I think, in these chapters. Buried sometimes, but ready to burst through. Hoping this encourages you. You said some things that can best be discussed over peanuts and Coke. I'm looking forward to it. Fraternally, Jim. Perge!"

"Perge!" was an old fraternity mystical tradition, something you put at the end of your letters to remind you of the bond that linked your souls; that friendship was not for college days alone. Usually I chuckled as I wrote it, feeling silly holding on to a trivial relic. Now I smiled as I read it. It stared back at me from the page a silent harbinger of things to come.

My 1929 TravelAir 4000 " Magic One"

FEBRUARY 1, 1970 (1)

"On the road of experience, and trying to find my own way, some-times I wish I could fly away. When I think that I'm moving, sudden-ly things stand still. I'm afraid because I think they always will."
JOHN DENVER

"Which way are they running?" I spoke in a calm, deep voice. It sur-prised me. I could not see them from 15,000 feet, running like fright-ened animals. In my mind's eye I saw them, clearly. I had them in a trap. Running into an ambush. I would turn them around and make them run the other way. Cut off their escape, walk the stick of bombs one by one down the road into them.

I am confident. This is it. Finally. I know my target is not a truck park, or floating oil drums. It is human beings, enemy beings, willing to blow me from the sky. I am a diving, screaming silver bullet, a college educated mind at the controls. I am the actor come to Life, thrust on stage. This is not rehearsal. There are guns to the north. Small arms fire directly below. My switches are set: Master Arm on, Fusing Nose and Tail, stations Select 1 and 5, Stick. All six Mark 82's will walk a path of TNT through the enemy. One by one they will separate from the wing racks in micro second intervals, the wires will pull from the bright brass clips on the nose of the fuses, loosing the tiny winged vanes to spin free in the wind and thus arm the bomb for impact. The bombs are green. Yellow striped bands just behind the nose. Cold to the touch. Rough hewn steel that explodes into slivers and shards , cutting down any flesh it meets. Ravaging all life in a 100 foot diameter. The concussion of its explosion will rip eardrums in heads it has not shattered. I never learn to love the bombs. I only love to be rid of them. They are a weight. Each a five hundred pound noose, an anchor to my high, fast flying. We drag them across the sky at 250 knots, cut them free in 450 knot forty five degree dives. They are crude, ugly, fat. But they will dive straight and true. I intend to lay them right up the road, across the smoke Nail 5-3 has dropped. The road crew is running. They have but a few more steps to take. I lock on the smoke.

A KIND OF MENTAL TATTOO

The white wing of the Bonanza glinted in the afternoon sun. Michigan below was blotted by carefully sculptured cumulus. The engine noise made conversation a chore and I chose to let it filter through my mind, recalling so many hours in the air, so many familiar landscapes. Jim was the pilot today, at the controls of an adventure he had talked about for a long time. I looked across the cockpit to his familiar silhouette, the windows of the Bonanza framing him in a still-living picture of determination. His glasses perched where they had always been, focusing the images of life which for him seemed always so clear. But that was why I had given him my manuscript to read. I wanted strong reaction, wanted candor and had gotten it. But I was also afraid of what he might say this weekend.

The manuscript was stuffed in with the camping gear in the baggage compartment. In the rear seat, peering out side windows, were two little people Jim and I had helped bring into the world; Katie and Scott. This adventure was for them, a weekend in northern Michigan camping along the Au Sable (Ah-Saw-Bow)River. The children were primed for the next two days. The flight to the camp was only the first leg, one to get over with quickly. The weather was spectacular for us, the air a cerulean blue. A sky I had come to know so well.

"Beautiful isn't it?" he said, turning his head to look out the left side. It was almost an off-hand remark, not really a question but the kind that floats into a conversation at altitude as oxygen must to sustain life.

"Yeah. How about a slow roll, to kinda juice things up?" I shouted across the cockpit. He turned back towards me with a wry smile. He would no more slow roll a Bonanza than an airline Captain a 707...

But I deeply suspected he probably wanted to.

"You Navy pilots never get that out of your system. Take any airplane and put it upside down if you can. On airways, in the middle of a stack of aircraft, anywhere, whenever it feels right!" He laughed as he said it. Turning serious then, he added, "We're making good time...look at that ground speed readout."

My bones ached a little as my right hand quietly moved a ghost control stick back ever so lightly and pushed against my left thigh. My mind had us upside down, arcing comfortably across lower Michigan, the green of the fields swirling—merging with the blue white of our crystal sky. Jim did not know the joys of aerobatics but he knew numbers and he knew people. I had known him well enough to prod him into dating Susie, the perfect girl for him. Now, twelve years later, we were entertaining the products of our marriages. The rocks and boulders life had put in our separate paths seemed grains of sand at the moment.

"Yeah, that tailwind is doing its thing. Ought to put us in there about 15 to 20 minutes early." I spoke the words and let them die in the droning cockpit. How easy it is, I thought, to drift away from the moment, back to yesterdays. Now, living in Fort Wayne, Jim and Susie as cross town neighbors, kids, barbecues, peanuts and coke and feet propped up on the coffee table discussing world affairs. Sometimes Jim was tired, sometimes a hint of impatience. This flight, this weekend, was designed to clear the cobwebs wound through us everyday by thoughts of security. I peered through the plastic window that separated me from wind and earth and absently wondered what it was that brought me here, whose farm below that might be with dark blue silos and white frame house and long green windbreak. I glanced over at Jim, all business again, saw him switching radio stations and twisting the knobs that would keep us perfectly on course. I trusted him and did not bother to check a thing.

Soon, easing the throttle back, Jim lowered the nose for the last leg

15

into the camp. Grayling, Michigan is 20 miles to our west. Interstate 75 is pointing north, a ribbon of white concrete with black ants crawling on it. The camp has its own runway, a grass and dirt affair long enough for twin engine King Airs. I have never seen it from the air and begin to search the ground for the first sign of it, an orange windsock fluttering beside a clearing.

"We just follow the river east out Grayling and that highway down there. The strip is between the road and the river about halfway. Its also 095 degrees 21 miles off the VOR." Jim was scanning out ahead, expecting to lock on the spot any moment. My manuscript flashed across my mind as we crossed the Interstate, lower now where I could see the cars. One was towing a long trailer. I thought perhaps it was a sailplane trailer. I thought again how I had almost died in Missouri in a car with a sailplane trailer hitched to it. When I wrote about it, I did not know why at first. My brother read it, said he liked it, but wondered how it fit into my story.

"There she is!" he said, pointing to the right of the nose. I quickly picked it up as Jim began a swing to the left. He would fly down the length of the runway first, checking for potholes, timber or deer. The kids were rubbing sleep glued eyes and stretching their necks to see everything they could. This was the exciting part for them. For us too, really. Reaching a goal, returning to earth, leaving the sky for now. A transition that seems so simple but for me is so profound.

"I've got a deer at the far edge. Probably no problem if he stays there, huh?" I looked for agreement from Jim and he nodded once he spotted the animal. The windsock gave us a light crosswind from the west, hardly much to even think about. Jim flew down the length of the runway eyeballing the turf. As he pulled up to put us on the downwind leg of our landing pattern, what I had written settled before me in a pattern I suddenly recognized...

I smiled as we turned final...in my opening chapter; a nurse; a night; I was still alive. And a Radiance of Light I was learning to understand.

Jim dropped the flaps another notch. We said nothing now. He was busy courting the runway ahead, judging the angle, anticipating the flare. The once flat earth grew trees and low hills into my conscious-ness. Extraordinary how proportions change in that brief moment before the wheels touch planet again.

Then suddenly we are wheel noise and metal straining and flurry of motion as the transition is made. "Nice one Post," I said, not too shabby for a civilian trained." A golden silence filled the cabin as we paused on the runway before spinning around to taxi back beside the woods closest to the river. The deer was gone; the pine trees stood nonplussed in silent welcome and only the haze of dust from our landing drifted off downwind. Another brilliant moment caught in my web. I filled my life with them it seemed. My manuscript was that. Full of fragments of my life. Dreams and penciled notes to my-self. Perhaps that was all they should ever be, I thought, notes to my-self. Maybe I was too caught up with ME. Maybe...and I noticed the smile across Jim's face. The kids were loose and had their heads pushing forward between us, eager to see everything.

"Easy, come on Katie, sit back, we're just going to park it down near the end." Jim said it kindly, the words not indifferent to the excite-ment in his daughter's mind.

"Dad, can we go fishing first?" Scott asked. He was fairly bursting.

"Well, we'll see," I said. "Plenty of time for everything." I said it with assurance, believing it to be true.

The river wound toward the lodge in curves and tucks that told no one its destination. The current was swift, the water clear. Where it battered rock, the churning voices seemed to echo from our distant past. We walked the path toward the main lodge, the kids dancing on ahead.

"I'm glad we planned this," he said. "You just gotta get out like this now and then, you know "

"Its great to see the kids so excited. They never forget weekends like this, carved out of Ordinary Existence," I said.

"You know," he said, "in your manuscript I got that feeling, that those years were carved out of your life. Or were they carved into your life, a kind of mental tattoo?"

"Both. A sculptor uses up his life carving things out of something."

"Well," he began, " I think your manuscript is good. Good carvings." He smiled.

It was pleasant to hear that, walking here beside the Au Sable. The warm feeling in my stomach was different today than it had been when we sailed for Vietnam. As we brushed aside tree branches across our path, Jim moved ahead clearing the way. He seemed a metaphor for what I had learned about LOVE in the war. He was still leading the way along paths I had yet to travel.

The kids reached the lodge first. Built of massive logs by a crafts-man, the place had all the warmth of heaven and a quilted down com-forter. I looked at it with reverence. All homes should be log I thought. With laughing children clamoring on the front porch and the river an arms length away. The caretaker's Black Labrador retriever bounded down the path to greet us, his tail wagging.

"Hey Jim, the place looks fantastic!"

"Yeah we love it up here. Wait'll you see the inside," he grinned.

It was a big place. Big enough for corporations to send a pack of ex-ecutives and wives for the weekend. But it was all ours this time. I discovered I could almost stand up in the fireplace. The player piano had roll after roll stacked on top of it. The kids wanted to fish. I wanted to build a fire and roast marshmallows and belt out tunes on the piano. But it was a good time for brown trout in the Au Sable. First things first.

We put our lines in at a bend in the river, upstream of the lodge.

"It's times like this," Jim began, "that I wonder what it is all about. As I was reading your book I got to thinking how differently things work out from the way we think they're going to. You, writing a letter and a book to your boys so they won't get trapped into wars; me, worrying when it all could end for me."

"I worried how I was going to end up, in Vietnam. Plenty. When I wrote about 'Bear Smith' I was thinking about that part of us that refuses to die...that's prepared for every emergency."

The kids were more hungry for food then they were for fish. The trout didn't take the bait and outlasted the patience of our young pair of adventurers.

In the lodge Jim and I surveyed the stash in the refrigerator and made some hamburgers that resembled small mountains. Bug juice and carefully cut chunks of some old cake made it a meal. "Daddy, are you going to play the piano?" asked Scott.

I looked at him with a grin. He still thinks I can play the Piano. The only tunes I know are "Heart and Soul" and a few measures of "Claire de Lune" that my girlfriend in high school taught me. But I can play lots of variations of those two numbers and make it sound good. I told Jim and he laughed.

"After your book, I know why those are the only tunes you learned. They're the only ones that ever mattered to you. Just look at the titles!"

Jim always saw things in new ways. I shook my head in mild disbelief. "That's really strange. You know, I think you're right." I moved over to the piano and before I put on a roll I tried to teach Scott, perched beside me, to play a part of "Heart and Soul." He would have none of it, of course. All my best intentions, all the wonderful symbolism was scrubbed bare with his impatience. So I put on a Sousa march and cranked her up.

Jim danced with Katie, and marched around the lodge holding up a big fire poker like a drum major. Scott and I joined in behind and the four of us stomped across the polished wood floors in perfect cadence.

When we were done, we sent the kids to get some wood.

"Mags, I think you're book isn't really about a combat cruise on a carrier at all. You've got parts that maybe only another Navy pilot would understand or really get into. Still, I didn't mind them. I just wonder whether..."

"I worried about that. I tried to make it as honest as I could but when you are looking back, the honesty seems a matter more of perspective. It's like a casserole. Stick anything honest you want in it just so the thing smells good when you're done. That's all people remember. With a kind of literary after taste."

"Go get the manuscript" he said, "I want you to read a couple things out loud. I want to hear you say them."

I lumbered off to the bedroom wing of the lodge and brought the wrinkled manuscript back with me. It felt too heavy. It felt weighty enough though to be something. Jim spread it out on the giant wooden coffee table and searched through it for what he wanted.

"Here it is," he said, "read this chapter." He handed me the last chapter of the manuscript. I looked at it and a little beyond, quietly recalling the time I had written it. I let out a deep breath and began. "In my dream I am writing a letter. The letter is furious, filled with the toxins of time... I am talking to you February 1, 1970. Do you hear me? You have no hold on me. None. I am talking to you my victims. I LOVE you now and I loved you then...'"

As I read the words aloud, the air in the lodge closed in around me and the near world seemed to dissipate into a vaporous, floating mirage. Untouchable. Ephemeral. I was hearing my words from a far away place and they were bouncing off columns of cloud with a deep, reverberating echo. The sensation was pleasant enough but odd I thought. Portending something I wanted to express to Jim, but the words for it were not there. They did not exist. There was a lifeline to the future surrounding this space I was in but I could only feel it, not describe it. A part of me continued reading while this other aspect of my Being seemed utterly relaxed and confident.

Reading the words of the chapter forced me to hear them as I had never read them before. A simple exercise in space-time. They say it is the space inside a vessel that gives it meaning; the white space between the characters on a written page that give words their impact. It is the space between the nucleus and the orbit of electrons that helps define my body. It is the perception of time between events that I call my Life. And here, beside the Au Sable River twisting and racing along the Michigan backbone, a window to my soul was opening. It was right that it should be in a log cabin and in conversation with this true friend.

I finished the short chapter as the children came through the door loaded with firewood, their eyes peering over the tops of the logs they struggled with. Jim quickly jumped up to help Katie. I set the manuscript down and helped Scott lower his logs to the hearth. How sudden is the transition sometimes from reverie to urgent action. The war had seemed like that very often. A hot meal one moment, the next I was freezing while dive bombing over a jungle. The fire took a while to express itself with leaping orange flames and light. As it gathered strength Jim warmed to his thoughts.

"LIFE IS a LOVE story," he began. "but sometimes we forget it and sometimes we call it by different names. Learning. Teaching. Marriage. Sickness. It has as many titles as there are religions, as there are books ."

I looked into the flames dancing in the fire and remembered what I had been taught in survival training. Build a fire as soon as you are settled. A fire is your friend. It gives you warmth and it gives you light. The person you call Friend will always do the same, unconditionally.

"I have this image sometimes," I said, "of LOVE being like a magnifying glass held before my life. It has the power to enlarge the smallest details and make them sensible, and it has the power to focus the energy of LOVE to accomplish what needs doing. You know, Jim, in a way that's all I wanted to see for myself, how it all worked. See clearly what I was being taught. How I had allowed myself to become the pawn of others."

In the fire I felt a warm envelope of LOVE opening. I had opened letters from home after "mail call" on cruise and it was that same feeling that surged through me now. I put my head back on the over-stuffed pillow at the end of the couch and stretched out.

"Answers seem to change with time," I said. "What everyone wants is answers, but they have a hard time finding them unless the questions they ask are the right ones. I think the right questions are time-less but the answers change over a lifetime. You remember how it was about age 22 and we were madly in love with a young lady? The question I always asked myself was, 'Does she really love me, or many times, did I really LOVE her?"

"Today, thirty eight and married, where LOVE has been tested in the ringer of the real world, if I have to ask those questions of myself something must be wrong. I have invested a big portion of my life nurturing that LOVE but all along I would have been asking the wrong question really. It should have been in the very beginning, 'How can I best express my LOVE for this person?' If I ask that every day I can watch the answers change over the years; from the nature of the gifts I give to the time I spend helping her through physically difficult crises. By asking the right question I clearly see answers that work, that change and change me, that leave me feeling connected to the LOVE crisscrossing our Universe." My thoughts seemed to float up to the ceiling of the lodge. Jim nodded his assent, remaining silent briefly. Only the crackling of the fire and the children's voices from the kitchen could be heard.

"In your book," Jim began, "you talked about being in love with flying and in love with life, and still you felt some kind of betrayal, by others and by yourself. How does that relate to the right questions? How do you know when you are asking the 'right' questions?"

"I can only answer for me. The right question is the one that appears to be the very hardest to answer. Hardest because it seems to ask me to give up my dreams of what I want desperately for myself, so that the world of Loving Dreams can evolve more fully. It is a question that when I ask it, I know in my heart I am connecting to another human being. Asking it I feel as though I have let go of the myth I was clinging to; the idea that I act alone; the idea that I can do something like I did in Vietnam and not expect it to ruffle my neatly packaged life time-capsule. The right question then was 'How can I best express my LOVE for these people some are calling my enemies?' It was not the one I asked."

BLAM! The door to the kitchen slammed shut behind Katie and Scott as they proudly carried a tray of ice filled glasses, cans of Coke, and a bowl full of "peanuts in the shell." I laughed at the site of our two children delivering our conversation food. How far have we come I thought, since the Senior Study at Phi Gamma Delta? I shook my head and captured the moment in memory forever.

Sometimes when I spoke, the words seemed to rise from an inner reservoir of feeling that vented only on special occasions. Generally, the emotions lay quiet beneath a facade of self—assurance. I wanted to unlock whatever it was that held me in check. I was embarrassed to use the word 'love' most of the time. My manuscript showed me that. And I was still shy about using it in conversation. It bounced back at me in oddly filtered ways. It was twisted most often and it was my fault because deep within me I was still coming to terms with it, trying to understand it. Others were mirrors for me, of thoughts and ideas I bounced off them. And "LOVE" so often reflected back like some dreamy, convenient, sugar coated shell that had to do battle with "real" rocks, the kind we had to juggle in life. But something in the fire, in the atmosphere of the lodge, in the recollections of Radiance I had experienced now and then through life kept me hostage. There seemed to be a Light coming through the cracks of a door ajar and it was stronger than any darkness that I had ever known. There were no shadows with this Light.

Jim seemed to understand. He sidled over to the player piano and put on an old song that raised the rafters and left us all energized. "You know," he said a few moments later, "sometimes the best questions aren't even questions. They are 'actions' we take without thinking, only sensing they are perfectly right. Others will question the actions, but if you are a model of intuitionally right action, you are expressing yourself in your highest form. A lot of bullshit I guess, all of which means simply that what is hateful to you, do not do to your neighbor. Anything written beyond that is mere commentary."

I had a manuscript in my hand that suddenly felt like a feather. I had written once somewhere in a note to myself, that ideas are weightless and we write to give them weight. It dawned on me, sitting there facing the friendly fire, that LOVE is weightless too, but we try to give it weight by living. But if LOVE and ideas are weightless, there was no reason to feel their "weight" and drag them like anchors through life. I looked at Jim and the kids silhouetted in front of the fire and silently asked my inner Being a normal, dumb question, "Where the hell was all this leading me?"

The conversation continued and was worth a bagful of peanuts and two icy Cokes. The kids discovered some hidden board games and parked themselves in front of the warm fire. The weekend settled into two long nights and flapjack breakfasts, paddling down the Au Sable in Grumman canoes, tossing sticks into the river for the Black Lab to retrieve until he was exhausted, whittling totem poles and making paper airplanes to fly inside the lodge. The piano got a workout and our fishing lines tangled once or twice. It was a LOVE story and it wasn't written anywhere but in smiles, children's smiles and fathers weathered memories of their own childhood. We were all children again along the Au Sable.

As the Bonanza lifted off the long grass strip Sunday afternoon, an orderly progression of images from the weekend and my manuscript trotted across my consciousness. We climbed away from the earth through a shallow layer of broken cloud into the bright sunlight where I put on my sunglasses. We banked south on course for home and I thought of Alison and baby Ryan at home, waiting for us. Another LOVE story at the end of our journey it seemed, always patient and expectant. Everywhere I looked I was experiencing LOVE. Washing it with this clear liquid that seemed to flow into every vision. I thought of carrier pilots reclining in Ready Room seats now, dreaming of home and family. It had seemed to me, once, that I could only be free if I were off the carrier, home from the war. Free to determine for myself what I could be. It was both true and a grave mistake. Choices I had then I have now. The pilots poised to fly those beautiful birds strapped to flight decks around the world at this very moment are free to write the beginning chapters of their own lives or the last chapter of the planet's. The illusion that touches us is one of our own making: that we are separate from one another in ways that matter. We are not! And plotting attack routes to Russia and China for a dreary nuclear mission the squadron skipper tells us he hopes we never fly is an antiseptic absurdity. If there is glory in any war, it is only in books. There is no Joy in it. There is no romance in killing other human beings. Where I denied LOVE, I left a scar.

I gazed down at Michigan and across the cockpit to my friend flying us Home. "Share it," he said with a smile. "Thousands write their stories but never tell them." The manuscript sat in a manila folder wrapped in a rubber band on my lap. I knew the first page by heart. I nodded my head and smiled back at my friend. "Some year," I said to myself, "I will." But I did not believe it.

All I saw were fragments. Bits and pieces of LOVE.

THE MANUSCRIPT
FEBRUARY 1, 1970 (2)

"I advise you to break to the South. Break to the South. We have 37 millimeter guns to the North. You can expect small arms fire."

Nail has spoken. I will run in east to west and turn port, South.

"Magic Three is in hot."

"Rog. and they're runnin, so come and get em' boys."

Nail is serving up the road crew like so many flapjacks.

"Come and get 'em boys!" It's his job. Spot the enemy, call in the bombers. You do it long enough, stay high, jink every five seconds, and you get to go home, or the war ends. Either way you win. It's a test of endurance. You and the sky and silver bullets aimed at you. Today the menu is road crew.

I'm looking good. The computer is locked on the smoke. It will ripple my bombs right where I want them. Down the center of the road, through Nail's smoke. The airspeed flickers past 450 knots. I close on 10,000 feet. Everything is perfect. The pipper is tracking precisely. It is time...NOW! My right thumb mashes the bomb pickle. In my headset there is a loud tone. Familiar. As long as I hold the pickle, I have the tone. It is a mournful, wavering dirge. Each time I release my bombs I am subjected to this brief executioner's song. It signals a change of consciousness. A 3,000 pound burden lifted and lost for all time. Strangely, it is a welcome sound when I am pointed towards the earth in a steep dive, flaming along at 450 knots. With it I begin to suck on the "g's," reaching for a positive four "g" pullout.

I feel the explosive kick release of my ordinance. It is thrown away from the triple ejector wing racks and my bird is shocked. She jerks upward, relieved of the drag and the weight. The fuel probe in front of the nose bobs up and down with a snap. Now I pull hard. Pull a solid 4 "g's" or I will sag low and be in the range of the rifles and slingshots aimed at me. Lower, and I may hear the curses and the crying of the road crew. My own Mark 82's exploding could lick the belly of my A4, torch my fuel tank, or scrap my engine. It is too dangerous down low. The "g's" will suck me back to my sky, to my element.

It is great fun to pull off a target. To get the nose up high and rack the bird up on a wing, put some "g" on again, bend around to look back at my hits. I am pulling, slowly releasing the "g" now, and I can see back two miles below me, the smoke of my six Mark 82's. I take a deep breath to replace the one I held during my dive.

"Three is off, Winchester." All my bombs are gone.

Nine point three seconds after the tone has ceased, Nail transmits.

"Heeeyyyy, NICE."

The green ugly fat yellow nosed spinning fused and armed whistling shrieking gifts of TNT leave no trail in the air. An invisible thread links them to me, to this day, this moment, Forever. Nine seconds, 10,000 feet, 450 knots, 9,000 miles from home, a clear and sparkling day, I am touched for the first time. I am certain I have killed.

Knee board card from February 1, 1970

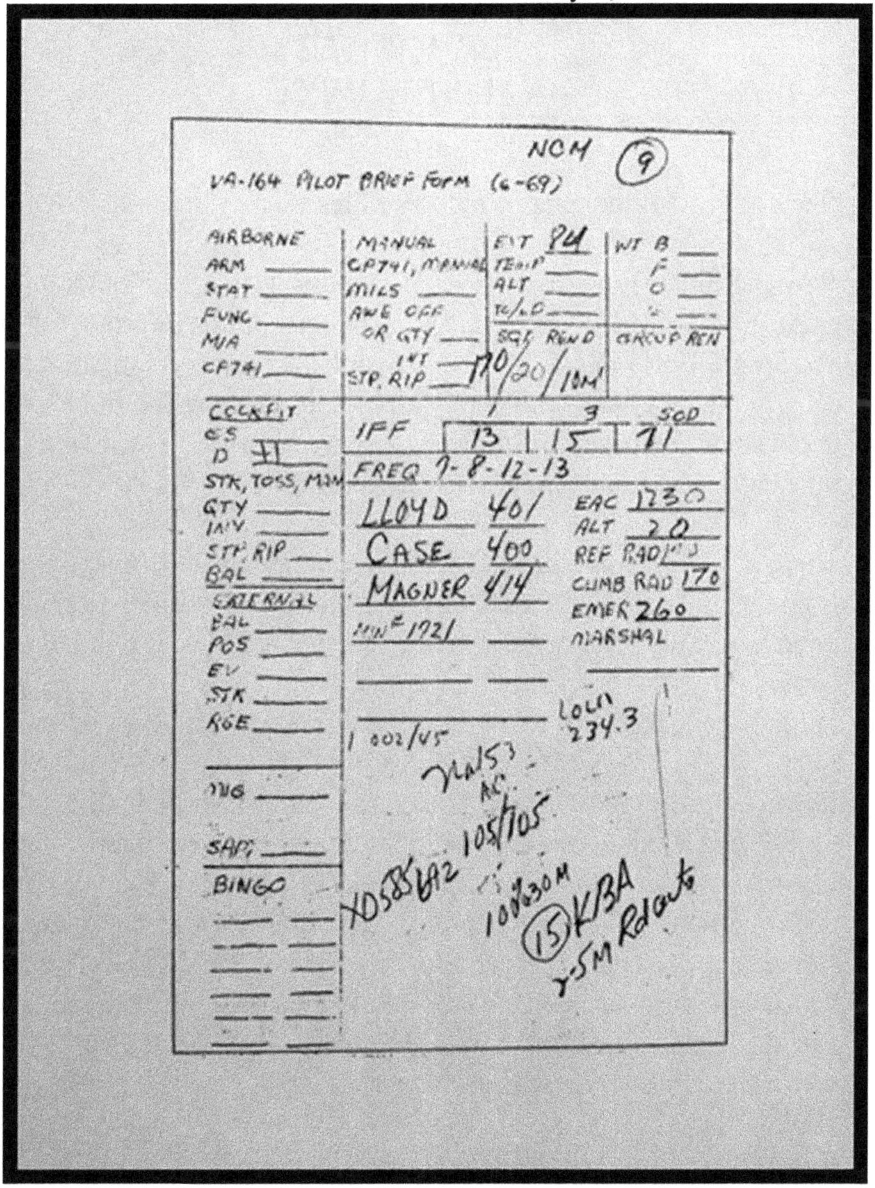
NCM (9)

VA-164 PILOT BRIEF FORM (6-69)

AIRBORNE
ARM
STAT
FUNC
M/A
CP741

MANUAL
CP741, MANUAL
MILS
AWE OFF
OR GTY
1ST STP, RIP 170/20/10M

EXT 84
TEMP
ALT
T/O

WT B
F
O

SEC REND
GROUP REN

COCKPIT
CS
D 71
STK, TOSS, MAN
GTY
INV
STP, RIP
BAL
EXTERNAL
BAL
POS
EV
STK
RGE

ING

SAP

BINGO

IFF 13 15 71
FREQ 7-8-12-13

LLOYD 401
CASE 400
MAGNER 414
MN 1721

EAC 1230
ALT 20
REF RAD
CLIMB RAD 170
EMER 260
MARSHAL

LOW 234.3

SUMMER 1960
A FIRST GLIMPSE

One Thirty AM: Interstate 40, thirty Miles west of St. Louis, MO.

Now the highway patrol officer is suggesting that I lie down in the grass. I will not. I insist I am OK. Snatches of conversation tell me Mr. Smith, Bob's father, is dead. Instantly. A miracle I am alive. One dead in the other car. One barely alive. Can I ride in the front seat to the hospital, between the attendants, someone asks? It will be a long time before a second ambulance can get here. Yes, I insist.

There are two people in the back of the ambulance. Bob and a man from the other car. I am nauseous, weak now. Bob asks in a voice tortured and slow, " Is my father Ok?" I cannot tell him. It will take two hours to pry the wreckage from around him. He is dead, gone. Your father is gone Bob, but I will deny it to him over and over.

The man next to him in the ambulance is badly mangled. He is sliced as if a cookie cutter has cut him open across his head; there is blood in every contour of his face. He reeks of alcohol. Has someone emptied a bottle of whiskey over him? The sight and the smell turn my stomach in deep convulsions. I lay my head on the attendant's shoulder; it is so heavy now. Bob asks of his father. I have no answer my friend. I cannot speak of it now. I remain silent. He asks in a voice soft with LOVE. "Where is my father?"

It is thirty miles to the Washington, Missouri hospital, run by Nuns in blue habits. They wash me out with alcohol; it is excruciating. They ask me my name and a flurry of questions. Looking at the ceiling, I see no need for any of it. I have just come from a dead place. Must we fill out questionnaires? Does the business of life include paperwork while there is still blood on the gurney?

There is a young Nun, a ray of light in this dark hour. She talks softly and holds my hand. In her eyes is a LOVE brighter, more enduring, more mysterious than I have ever known. Her softly chiseled face is framed by a radiant white border. In the three days I am in her hospital, two nights we spend sitting beside the open third floor window, the Missouri summer clinking wind chimes in the courtyard below. I have long forgotten the words of our conversations, but never their effect. I wanted to say that I loved her very much. That she had something, a LOVE, I could not touch, that we seemed from very different worlds, yet lived in the same one. I wanted to say that I loved her. And finally I did. I did say it. Said it but qualified it... Subscripted to this time, this place. Here, now. For what you are doing, for me... The night drew around us close. Her face was reflecting the light from the courtyard, barely discernible in its dimness. She took my hand in her's and said nothing. We spoke not a word for an eternity. Only the wind continued its conversation.

I flew home aboard my first jet, a Convair 880. In the cockpit I remember the feeling of sitting astride the point of a pencil slicing through space. The glory of July's anvil cumulonimbus cathedrals stood in stark relief against the quilted farmland below. I wanted this view to last forever, to fill my life with joy. I wanted to LOVE and be loved and live my dreams. I was Certain I would and a car wreck in the summer of my sixteenth year could not end them.

The A4F Skyhawk flown from the USS Hancock 1969-1970 with VA-163 and VA-164

PASSING UNDER THE GOLDEN GATE ENROUTE TO THE GULF OF TONKIN

SUMMER 1967

NAVY FLIGHT TRAINING

YOU ARE A LESSON IN TIME

The car sailed quietly over the black two lane backwoods road that ran north between Meridian and Starkville, Mississippi. Weekends were mine. To drive one hundred miles north and strap myself into a single seat sailplane. I loved the flying. No instructors to critique me, no debrief, no mission plan. All that was necessary was thermal heat. To soar alone above the green carpet forests of Mississippi, alone with the great buzzards and hawks.

Early on Saturday morning; horse drawn buckboards headed into town, dusty brown feet of children swinging off the rear of the beds. I smiled at them, slowed, waited my chance to pass. Wanted to stay there, slow, dreaming with them as they bounced in unison, heads moving side to side; eyes questioning me, lips smiling. I am a jet pilot you know... We are traveling this world at such different speeds; here in my Pontiac, you on your gray old buckboard, me with twin speakers, you with ears to the natural world. I have slowed to join you, will you speed up ever, to be with me in my world? The buggy pulls off to one side when it can. I toot and pass and wave in my mirror. They have time to think. They slip through life on the slow wheel of time and fortune, I spin through on a hot turbine, leaving residue and noise. But I do love you Mississippi. Your kudzu green and red orange earth rolling away hills dark starry nights. Tin shacks on stilts, dusty red barren yards smoke curling from chimneys. You are a lesson in time, in poverty of "things" yet rich in natural pine forests. I cannot speed past the farmer plowing wind and earth with a single blade behind a sweating horse the sun rising over his shoulder. You there, I am going to fly a sailplane today, for hours. I will soar above this earth you carve so carefully. I will etch lines of effort in the sky while you create the patterns of ribboned earth I use for palette. We are both conspirators, both actors on this stage we have set up for re-hearsal. I want to know the feel of the earth, the soil in my hand, my fingernails black with dirt. You want to fly, to join the column of sky that holds a promise of freedom. Perhaps we should talk, share these dreams of ours.

I could not know that this day I would nearly die in a thunderstorm. Smashed and battered by my own stupidity. Whipped and lashed by wind, my ship holds together, her wings taut. It is all I can do to land her in the teeth of the storm. Friends run and grab the wings. I have been foolish. And that evening, I will recount with a date from the college in Starkville, the thrill of the day; build an image I must maintain for sanity, and for years to come. I drift home the way I came. Past poverty, past beauty, past the past. When will life begin to make sense? I am so full of life, trapped by its anomalies, but eager to learn her secrets. And there, there ahead is another buggy, life plodding along behind it. Would they pick up a hitchhiker... me? I could park the Lemans forever, learn the guitar, walk the hot summer back roads, plant corn, watch the buzzards soar, weather the storms under a corrugated roof. Sweat, get thirsty, drink red pop, listen to the preacher, fish the Tombigbee. Old muddy river twisting through Life. Tell me, please, just whisper it... why do I fly; what is it I LOVE; where are you taking me?

FEBRUARY 1, 1970 (3)

Nail 5-3 repeats it. Niccceeee." My hits are excellent.

"Ok, ah number two, put yours further down the road, please."

Magic One "rogahs" Nail and Bullet Bob cranks the A4 around to get in position for roll in. Now that there is a jungle full of smoke he can see the target. Poor ol' Bullet. Leftover from the PBY Navy; ancient flying boats with coffee and donuts. The Skyhawk is quick and tight, and fortunately very forgiving. Bullet is usually in the last county and today it's another world. The target simply eluded him with his oatmeal vision. But he is a good guy. And a good bomber. A Lieutenant Commander who is big and soft and writes his wife and kids every day. She writes him every day too and Mick ribs him every time a letter from Flora Jean hits the mail call. "Hey Bullet, is FLORA JEAN still hot for your bod—de?" he cackles. But I always wonder to myself why in the world he is here, here in this screaming jet, gut wrenching world.

He makes his run while I loft up to a perch for another one. Case is ready at his end of the circle, this time with the guns. He reminds Bullet, "Cameras." He never forgets to remind us. Turkey is beautifully methodical. The cameras are on the belly of the aircraft, facing aft. They click away automatically as we pull off target, photographing the hits in glossy black and white. The spies on the ship want nice clear evidence of the potholes we make in the jungle. Our biggest problem is remembering to flip the switch on. We designate someone to remind us. I have gone days without a photo. For some reason I don't really care.

Bullet is pulling off target now. I flip the gun switch to ARM and rotate the gunsight to adjust the pipper to the proper setting. I do it all automatically while something sitting on my shoulder is whispering politely in my ear. Not too loudly. In fact, barely intelligibly. I glance back at the smoke over my shoulder and tighten my turn some. No time now for reflection. This is a THING. This is NOW. I don't want to blaze down the run in, squeeze the trigger and have dead silence. It's too embarrassing. The switches have to be right. There is a job to finish. We'll spray our hundred or so rounds of 20 mike mike in the crowd and and that'll be that. I won't see them, but they'll be there. Nail said they were runnin'. I think we slowed 'em up with the bombs, now we'll put the nails in the coffin. I'm going home with black smoke on the gun ports. Two years of flying Navy jets' and this is what I've trained for. I feel like a professional. The quiet voice on my shoulder sighs, is lost in the shrieking wind of my run in. The pipper dissects the rising smoke and dust and I squeeze the gun trigger. The guns burp and shake the aircraft. They spit and spit and the sound is dull, thudding. Nothing like the movies. Almost boring. I press the run, walking the rounds up the shoulder of the road where I can still see it. I am strafing and I'm fast and I'm getting low and the guns finally quit, exhausted. Pull up baby. PULL UP! NOW!

AUGUST 2, 1969

I WAIT FOREVER FOR CALIFORNIA TO DIE

SAN FRANCISCO. Goodbye Sweetheart. Goodbye dear thing that gave me Weekends. A white washed city in green overalls. Slipping out of my grasp. Friends waving a red blanket at center span of the Golden Gate. Tissue paper reeling out with the wind, floating, snagging high in the ship's radar antenna. I LOVE you All, this moment, this scene from the movie of my life. Starched white A4's cramming the flight deck, needle nosed, pointed away from home. I turn from the bow and thread my way slowly aft as the Hancock sails beneath the bridge.

The Golden Gate is orange. Very orange. The squadron color is also orange. We are the Ghostriders, on our emblem riding a great white stallion emblazoned with a diamond, a rainbow of color spewing forth. We are also ordinary men. Twenty pilots. Most of whom have slipped below to the Ready Room now, except for me. I have seen this film of me before. In it I must stand on the flight deck aft, as close to the edge as possible. To patiently witness the disappearance of California. To watch her sink. An execution by lethal injection.

The Hancock is churning the sea beneath her belly. The giant screws kick and claw the Pacific. The wind across the deck is fierce. I lean my body back into it, jam my hands into my pockets The continent sinks slowly. The towers Of the Golden Gate are sloshed by white Pacific paint. Between troughs they reappear, dripping, still upright. Someone has pulled the plug on my homeland. My nostrils burn in the acrid stack gas belching from the gut of the Hancock. I don't know that this is required. That I remain here watching this quiet burial. But I wait forever for California to die. Then stand on my toes to try and resurrect her. I cannot. I have been cutoff. Numbly, I begin to sense the curve of the earth, the enveloping vastness of the sea; the singular profound loneliness of a warship headed for destruction, sailing without Joy. My only friends this moment are these warbirds, sparkling in the Pacific sun. They are quiet, oddly serene; perhaps they understand.

I glance up at the ship's bridge. Has anyone been watching me? Asking why a pilot would stand so long on the fantail when only one thing matters now...Vietnam. Pilots are not supposed to question their mission aboard a carrier - just go with it.

The carrier sails West, against the subtle wishes of five thousand men. Nothing can stop it. Some implacable cosmic force drives her; it is pure inertia; absolute momentum. And with it, sail my dreams, my dread, whatever my life has become. Everything in my being is lashed to her throbbing hull. Each morning the gap between two realities will narrow. There is a knot in my heart, another jammed in my throat. I have chosen this. But I do not know why.

I spit into the sea. Watch it disappear and stare with vacant eyes at the carrier's wake, a greasy white slick trail fading to nothing in the direction of home. When the darkness of a theater is replaced by the bright light of day, heroes squint and squirm and write long letters home. Hiding themselves in nickel envelopes. Which of us will die on this cruise, I whisper inside? Will it come on the last cat shot on the final mission like it did for Rog Myers? Someone will not return, it is certain. I turn into the wind across the flight deck and move forward among the aircraft lashed with heavy weather chains. None of us will fly till Hawaii. There is that to look forward to. The Gulf is at least twelve days away. I make my way to Ready Four. Down the long escalator, threading through knee high hatches, ducking my head, silently reading labels on pipes and brass doorplates. Every small office reeks of coffee brewing. In the Ready Room is the Squadron Duty Officer, his chair tilted back, legs stretched across the duty desk. Lt. Mick Cael, smiling under his mustache. From Opportunity,   Washington. Our get drunk get funny pilot. A lovable comic actor pilot every squadron needs. "Maggot, where you been boy?"

AUGUST 30,1969

THE ANGEL HOVERS OVER THE SEA

"Aircraft in the water! Aircraft in the water!" The voice on the Ship's loudspeaker chills my nerves. The Hancock heels hard to port, rolls me against the bulkhead of my bed. My eyes are suddenly wide open, glassy. In the distance I hear muted, agitated voices, and the pounding of feet. I know it is not a dream.

Every emergency ditching procedure floods into my mind as I pour myself into my flight suit and boots...Who is it? Who the hell is it? I run for the closest hatch to the outside. I lean out from the starboard gun tub. The air is dead quiet. The ship now barely moving. Still turning hard starboard. Making a huge circle in the Gulf outlined by a line of white froth. In the near distance, the "Angel" hovers over the sea in a shower of spray. He must have spotted the pilot. But who is it?

Somehow it is comforting to think all this machinery can be turned so quickly into a rescue ship. There are several thousand sets of eyes peering over the side to spot you, helicopters whooping around like giant gnats. For a brief moment, the ship seems a compassionate friend, a girl I might like after all. For once she is not pushing relentlessly toward the war torn shore. She has paused, stopped for a breather, acknowledged us as human beings, as pilots. Maybe I can LOVE her. "Bear" Smith is in the water. His Skyhawk litters the Gulf of Tonkin bottom. On the catapult shot, a moment before he is launched, his engine begins to unwind, dropping rapidly in rpm. There is no time left to cry, "Suspend the starboard cat." He moves his left hand from the throttle and positions it on the emergency jettison handle. The catapult hurls him, engine failing or not, off the bow.

41

There is enough airspeed to pull up the nose, to jettison 3,000 pounds of bombs and a full centerline gas tank. There is just enough momentum to turn slightly away from the ship and check the engine instruments one last time. It is dropping through 40 percent. And then there is no time left. He reaches up for the ejection handle above his helmet and pulls it, hard

He is extremely low. But the seat and chute work. He is now a spectator, swinging madly under the chute for perhaps 3 or 4 seconds. The ship brushes past him, close, but far enough that he is not caught in its antennae.

As I stand in the gun tub, Bear is ready to be hoisted into the helo. For the experience, wetter, and wiser. And I am happy. Happy he is not "lost at sea." Bear is a favorite LSO (Landing Signal Officer). An unconventional one, a damn good one. His deep voice on the radio exudes absolute confidence. He will call me on the radio by name, calming jangled nerves if I am having difficulty getting aboard. All the official jargon is set aside. "Ok now Maggie, everything is alright. You were just a little high and fast that last time and the deck is pitching some, but keep her coming. I've got ya...a little left for line up...looking good...the deck is down, hold what you've got."

When he says "I've got ya," in his slow, baritone voice, all my anxiety drains away. If God had said it, I would not feel better. I take a deep breath, concentrate on the meatball, the angle of attack, the lineup. Fear is diminished to reasonable proportions, the question dancing in my brain, wondering why can't I land this bastard tonight. Two times I have missed the wires. I'm low on fuel, the weather is miserable. Deck pitching wildly. I've had vertigo for the last twenty minutes. This is absolute madness. Events turning sour begin to wind me up like a top. It's my turn in the barrel. Bear's voice cuts through the storm inside and I feel the pressure evaporate. He is going to reel me in like a big fish. There is no concern in his voice. Only total certainty. I settle into my seat, tug on my sweat soaked gloves to get them tight, adjust my feet on the rudder pedals and come Home, slipping down the glide slope as if it were nothing.

In my mask I quietly mutter a "Thank You" to Bear, shed the arrest-ing cable from my hook and taxi forward.

Now, standing in the gun tub, watching his rescue, I just smile. I think for him this war is just another day. A day to go flying, be calm, do what you have to do. He is so good at it. Sometimes it seems that way for me too. To do what I have to do...

DIARY NOTES

NUMBERS IN A CLOUD

September 28, 1969

..."Mail Call, Mail Call"...The loud speaker signals a lifeline being flung my way. I go wild in anticipation. The Duty Officer flips letters across the Ready Room seats and we dive for them. In a minute, everyone is sitting, reading, silent, chuckling softly. A spell descends upon us. The letters are a healing balm, linking us to a life and a LOVE an eternity away from our watery hell. Lord, it is wonderful to get a letter! Today I did not. In my chest a wounded bird flaps around for as long as it takes to die. I just go about my business, hoping the next mail call is soon. It may be days...

October 9, 1969

...In the 0'Club, Cubi Pt., the Philippines; most everyone smashed. What a fantastic bunch of people. Pilots, men, boys, kids crazy about life, on sabbatical from an ugly dream. "Liberty" is what we live for. Joyous release from the tyranny of a flight schedule. Real food. Dirt. Women to look at! Across the harbor, Olongapo steams in the heat tonight. Kids are swimming in the putrid river that borders the base, begging for nickels from the sailors crossing the bridge that links city and base. Reflected in their eyes are the neon lights of "PO Town." When I get back to the ship, I have to shower to begin to feel human again.

October 29, 1969

To be touched by the war, something will have to happen to break through the smoke screen of numbers, days, dirty flight suits and Ready Room movies. I am an actor in this drama unfolding without a written script, yet everyone knows his Part perfectly. We have seen it all before in a hundred movies, in Victory at Sea episodes every day on the ship's TV. The smoking script leaves a haze of resignation across my mind, dulling the senses, blotting out light and energy...

In Flight Deck Control, a little shack under the island at flight deck level, an artist has grease penciled a picture of the Golden Gate on plexiglass, stuffing it between two very green hills. Just above it he has written, "Days Till Home," and under it is the white outline of a cloud with a number in it. I stare at it while I stand the Integrity Watch in the shack. Not until the number is below two hundred does it seem to change. In this cramped, humid space, the number becomes a slowly ticking metronome, a kind of mental water torture dripping across my consciousness. I peek in sometimes as I pass by to check the number, to lift my spirits. Is there a cloud above our lives, with a number in it? Who changes the number in it? To what grease penciled heaven will I return?...

November 8, 1969

..."Where you been Maggot?" Mick Cael leans back in the Duty Officers chair, a big shit eating grin from ear to ear. I have just returned tonight from a black niagara towering over the Gulf of Tonkin. My Skyhawk and I have wrestled certain death, wasted our bombs in the center of an enemy universe and there is nothing to show for this two hours of pure insanity. The typhoon season is upon us. But I laugh at Mick, a big cigar sticking from beneath his curling mustache.

"Mick," I sighed, "you know what I need right now?"

"Yeah," he cracks, "a Big Mac, order of fries, and a vanilla shake!" He was only half right, but it didn't matter.

"How'd you guess Mick?" The war according to Cael. Made as much sense as this night had. And my mouth began to water.

Where HAVE you been, Maggot? I asked myself. Worse, where are you headed?

FEBRUARY 1, 1970 (4)

Magic 3: (me) Roger, and threes in hot, I don't have you in sight.

Nail: Ok I'll be off to the north, you'll be clear.

Magic 3: Ok, clear.

Nail: Make it about 20 meters short now.

Magic 3: Rog.

Nail: And Magic One's in hot I'm tally on three and the FAC.

Magic 3: Threes off left.

Nail: Hey, real good, real good hit.

 Magic 2: Ah, two's overhead target takin' some pics.

Nail: Rogah.

Magic 1: One's off.

Nail: Roger one.

Magic 1: Ah, thiziz One, I got enough for one more run.

Nail: Ok, come on around. Two you're cleared in.

Magic 2: Ah, two's winchester.

Magic 3: Three also winchester.

Magic 2: Two I'll stay high, about 14 thow.

Magic 3: What's your posit two?

Nail: You got several good read cuts I can see now.

Magic 2; I'm west of the target...Just above the smoke.

Magic 1: One's rollin' in.

Nail: Ah rogah, just on the east end of the smoke, short of the smoke towards you.

Magic 1: One's off...and I'm winchester.

Nail: Ohhh Kay, I think I'll go down and see what happened.

Magic 2: Ah, One, I'm very high at your three.

Magic 1: Roger

The three of us rendevous in a wide circle over the target. Nail drops down, zigzagging over the trees to assess the damage. In exactly 59 seconds, he radios back our report card.

Nail: Ohhh Kay Magic Stones, looks like you did a pretty good job on those gomers there, I didn't see any out there runnin'. Why don't I go up there and take a little closer look with the binoculars and see if we can't get you some KBA on those.

 Magic 1: Rogah!

Case is still snapping pictures. Nail takes almost three minutes over the target. We climb to seventeen thousand feet in a tightening spin above the drifting smoke. Finally, he is ready with the BDA.

Nail: Okay Magic Stone, your target coordinates were Xray Delta 585692. I had you on at 1345, off at 55, gave you a hundred percent within 30 meters and because of, ah, the first man in, his bombs were RIGHT there, I'm gonna give you a possible 15 KBA, and you got two five meter road cuts.

Magic 1: Two five meter road cuts.

Nail, Ah, roger, and that's a possible 15 KBA.

Magic 1: Rog, thank you very much Nail.

Nail: Rog, THANK you, that was real good work!

Magic 1: Okay Magics, lets go button 20.

I have scribbled the numbers on my kneeboard, circling the number 15. I reach over and flip the UHF frequency to button 20.

Magic 1: HEY. good bombin'. Hey, I'm gonna... why don't you guys join up in formation here and let me take some pictures of you. I've got Gibson's camera here...and let me get a couple of pictures of for-mation. I'll go ahead and do the talkin' and let's head out about ah, one seven zero till we get a lock on somewhere.

A minute later, Hillsboro talks to us, then Vice Squad, as we report the BDA and begin a swing to the east to take us home. The air is smooth, our voices subdued. I have slid the pencil back in its spring holder on my knee pad. The eraser rests on the circled 15. I glance at it, look back outside to the land they call South Vietnam. I inhale slowly, deeply, thinking thoughts I hardly recognize. I push them off into space, drive them out with a check on my fuel state, a glance at my armament switches. Gotta be smooth now, Case is sliding over to fly tight formation...

Are there going to be no dead Ghostriders this cruise? Will there be only dead enemy?

NOVEMBER 12, 1969

DROWNING IN THE BLACK NIGHT

Full moon. Norwood is leading. Two of us tonight. I'm the happy wingman, listening and tagging along behind. Getting close to the target now.

Mike's lights flicker. Once, twice. Then go out. I know precisely what it means. His CSD has quit. He has no electrical power. I am the leader now. Mike will pull out his RAT (ram air turbine) to regain some electricity and we'll motor around for a Skyspot, drop our ordnance B-52 style from a safe and comfortable 18,000 feet and be done with the miserable work. I fly up beside him and take the lead.

We work like a team. We've briefed this a hundred times. Just follow me old buddy. I tell the world below of our problem, circle until we get the radar people to line us up for the drop. Mike comes up on his emergency hand held radio and shouts into it on Guard frequency.

"Magic, can you read me? Flash your lights if you do."

His voice sounds harried, a little wild. The background noise drowns him out. But the PRC 90 is working, though at the moment, we don't need it. We make our high altitude run in: switches set; "armstrong" the Master Arm, wait for the word to pickle. Twelve Mark 82's will be spewed across the black jungle from the black sky, bursting through the undercast and splitting the night in microsecond fury. It will be simple. Black death.

"Magic Stones, left one degree...standby to mark...hack hack." The radar ground controller spits out the command. My right thumb presses the bomb release the instant he says hack. Simple work tonight.

It isn't. Mine release. Norwood's airplane is in trouble. There is zero electricity. None. His bombs are still neatly arrayed on his racks. He is shouting at me on Guard, and the whole world can hear him. Voices rise up from the ether offering assistance. I don't want them now. Only Mikes. Then Norwood disappears. No voice, nothing.

I circle, lights bright and flashing. He must be somewhere out there! Please God, let him be. I make almost a full circle before I hear the hiss of his radio.

He sounds half panicked as he tries to fly and shout into his radio. I cannot see him even with the full moon. Finally, he slips onto my right wing from out of nowhere. I roll out headed Northeast, a course that will take me across Danang and toward the Hancock. The next decision is not so easy.

He cannot land aboard the ship if he cannot jettison the bombs. He could possibly try to land at Danang, but that is going to be rough without electrical power. No gear indications, nothing. The other option is to fly by the ship and eject, throw away the airplane, hope we can find him in the water.

I radio the Hancock to get "Combat Carl" Bruntlett on the radio. He is the resident A4 expert. He is also a flaming nerd about it. But now, I want, I need him. His thousands of hours in A4's may yield a solution. Norwood hangs on my wing. It takes forever to get Combat to the radio.

Norwood signals with his flashlight that he is getting low on fuel. My own fuel state is fine, and even allowing for the extra drag of his bombs, his should not be critical. Yet, that is unmistakably his signal. He wants to do something NOW!

Just then, "Combat" comes up on the air. "Magic Stone. Bruntlett here. Whats the problem?" I recognize his voice, sigh a little thinking now I've got the Natops Manual on the radio with all the answers.

"Norwood has no juice. Can't tell if the rat is out. Looks like it is but it's hard to tell. He can't unload his bombs, they're all still hanging. Have we got ANY way to get rid of those things if he doesn't have electrical power?"

"Negative. Even to jettison he has to have some power."

"He's just signaled he's low on fuel. I'm still fat. And he wants to know if he's going to eject at the ship or land at Danang?"

Combat, in all his wisdom, decides we should try to land at Danang. Take the arresting gear. See what happens. He'll be fast, overweight, not even certain his gear is down and locked. It seems an incredible risk, but maybe it is better than getting wet, then drowning in the black night beside your carrier.

I say so long to Combat, switch frequencies, raise Approach Control at Danang. They know about the emergency. They've been listening on Guard. This will be my first time into Danang. The weather is sick. Raining, low ceiling, the approach from the north invaded by karst peaks.

"Danang Approach, Magic Stone 404, flight of 2 alpha fours: base Plus 5, two zero zero twenty two off Danang."

Danang Comes up quickly. "Magic Stone, Danang- Radar Contact."

"Roger. Magic Two has serious electrical problems. A full load of six Mark 82's unable to jettison. Requesting section approach immediately, two will take the short field gear, please have the crash crews standing by. Magic Two is indicating low state, over."

If Mike is truly low on fuel, he might flameout any moment. I have to believe he is still fat on fuel. So I will fly the full approach, try to be smooth, get him down on the "ball," drop him off and pray he doesn't blow up on the runway. He tucks up tighter on my right wing and we start down.

I decide to dirty up before we enter the cloud deck. It means we will use more fuel, but it will be easier for him to drop the gear and flaps in the clear air and if he has problems, to stabilize with me before we hit the klag.

Approach sheperds us around to the North and lines us up for a long straight in. They repeat the fact that we if we get low on the glide slope we will bore two holes in Vietnamese mountains. I thank them for the friendly advice.

The gear and flaps come down simultaneously. I watch Mike bob and dance a little, then snuggle back up on the right wing. His gear appears down, but in the dim light it is impossible to be sure. At least he has drag out there and he is still with me. We drop into the clouds that hang for 7,000 feet below us.

The turbulence begins to increase. The rain spatters the windscreen in great fits and slugs. I am flying fast. Purposely. I am certain I am jerking the plane all over the sky. I look back and he has disappeared. I strain my neck but I cannot see him anywhere. On either side. He is not in my mirrors. The turbulence is vicious. I have only one choice — to continue.

I drop slightly low while searching for Mike. Ease it back up to the glide slope. And continue. This is madness. Do I have a wingman or don't I? He cannot talk if he is flying beneath me. He cannot talk if he has lost me. Without me there is only ejection. I am his only reference to right side up. I am his attitude gyro, his only link to a longer life. If you're with me Mike, please hang on. We are getting close.

"You're approaching the glide slope Magic Stone, begin descent...
You're up and on glide slope, now 3 miles from touchdown..."
Danang is working us nicely. I hope there is an US. I listen and fly
and wait.

The clouds begin to fragment, brush past the canopy like fleeting
ghosts. Suddenly they rise above me. I am clear. There is 600 feet
between my A4 and the jungle.

I look back in my mirrors. There is a tail, a beautiful thin gray tail
sliding to my right. Mike's A4 materializes again on my starboard
wing. He has been flying under my tailpipe.

The "ball" is bright orange, sharp and clear in the corner of my windscreen. I put it between the green datum lights and line up with the
centerline strobes. It is time to kiss him off. I flash my wing lights
and turn gently left. Mike says nothing. He bores straight ahead, descending. I am sure he has the lights and the runway in sight. If not, I
need to be somewhere close. There is no way around the pattern
without me. I throttle back and descend slightly, well off his port
wing.

When he contacts the runway, there is brilliant shower of sparks. His
tailhook is dragging across the cement like a giant flint. He appears
to be in the center of the runway and suddenly he slows. The hook
has grabbed the Baker short field arresting gear, and held. By the
book, his A4 should be stretched like a piece of licorice, or rolled up
in a blazing ball trailing cable ripped from a failed brake drum. But
he is down, in one piece it seems, and it feels good. I jam the throttle
up and accelerate.

There is not enough time to return to the Hanna and land in the cycle.
I circle Danang one more time, shoot another gloomy approach, land,
and park next to Norwood's airplane on the revetment. He is all
smiles.

His CSD was inop and the ram air turbine was corroded shut, useless. Three more of the aircraft checked aboard ship will turn up the same problem. And he had plenty of fuel. Our coded flashlight hand signals didn't work too well tonight! We stand in the dark rainy night beside our aircraft, two carrier pilots lost on a sea of wet concrete, telling each other how sweet it is to be somewhere safe, even if there is a goddamn war going on over the hill.

I watch the silhouette of Mike as he saunters off to the Line Shack fifty yards away. Mike has the most beautiful wife in the squadron — Bev. He is still alive and that's the way it ought to be. They have postponed having children until he completes his combat tours. It looks like he will.

My Skyhawk sits patiently beside me, cooling in the rain. Does she know more than I do about our futures?

NOVEMBER 24, 1969

STRANGE LONELY MOMENTS

Today I fly the Barcap Tanker — launch and fly North towards the coast and Haiphong to find our two air wing F8's flying figure eights. Their mission is to protect the fleet from Migs. There haven't been any for months, but that's probably only because it would be politically irresponsible. The Crusaders pilots are the creme-de-le-creme of fighter pilots, or so they like to remind you. And they are thirsty bastards, happy to suck every pound of fuel I have and let me flame-out halfway home to save their own necks.

The first problem is to locate them. Radar helps. But we are on opposite sides of a big rendezvous circle and it takes time and fuel to finally get them in trail, reel out the drogue and get them plugged in. They have to slow to 250-260 knots and that just kills them. Sticking their fuel probe into the slipstream adds enormous drag and at 260 knots, the fuel drogue likes to dance in the wash behind my aircraft. Makes it a very tough target for them, and today they get agitated. I curse them under my breath and let them flail around. I'm doing my job. They can't stick their probe where it belongs, that's their problem!

When the task is complete, they have used as much JP-4 as I have given them. The two fighters coolly thank me and flame off to the North for some last figure eights. They're real good at that. I'm good at reeling in the drogue and diving for the layer of stratus cloud layer several thousand feet below me.

There is nothing I enjoy more than long slow aileron rolls. The thick layer of stratus below me stretches maybe one hundred miles back toward the ship. I drop down to kiss the clouds, tickle the tops with my belly tank, pull the nose up and roll inverted, hold it until the nose sinks back through the horizon, then roll wings level as I sag into the wisps again. Once I begin the sequence, I won't quit. It is a beautifully exquisite feeling to sense the speed, the little knot of turbulent energy in the cloud, bounce out and curve up, and slow as a minute hand roll upside down, hold one positive "g" and arc across this blue white paradise all reserved for me.

At the top of a roll, inverted and deep in reverie, my radio crackles to life. Piraz, code name for the radar ship somewhere below me, calls to confirm my mission complete.

"Magic Stone, mission complete?"

"That's affirm."

"Roger, your pidgeons Rampage one seven zero, sixty five. Magic Stone, is pilot's name Magner?"

I bolt to life. He has just said my name over the air where the whole enemy world can hear it. And how does he know my name? Does he know I'm doing aileron rolls in a tanker A4 when it's against the rules? I am shocked out of my blissful sleep. Then just as suddenly I realize who has called my name. Dan Pence! It can only be. "Dan, is that you," I ask incredulously.

"Roger. How are you?" "Hey, I'm great. How goes it down there?"

"Real good. Not bad at all. Just keeping tracka you birds, zabout it."

"Hey, its great to hear your voice out here. Sorry I can't come down and give you a good show. Kinda cloudy ."

"Yeah, that's alright. Next time. Take care. Maybe see you in Cubi."

"Rog. Don't get seasick! Go Blue... Magic out."

I am stunned, but smiling. Pence and I muddled through NROTC together at Michigan. Now, here in the middle of nowhere, in a war, two years later, his voice echoes from the past into the present. I see him standing in front of North Hall, chin tucked in, sword vertical, ordering platoon leaders to "Report!" He is the Company Commander. Destined for great things. How long ago it seems; Ann Arbor, Saturday's. I don't even know which day it is here. But I am flying, and I've always wanted to do that. Always wanted the solitude of flying alone, my own jet. Years of dreaming, models turning in the air over my bed, shadows in the morning light on the wall beside my pillow. Always wanted to fly --never thought of this though. War. Strange lonely moments frozen in memory, pinpoints on a map of life. My name floating up from the sea. Arriving in my headphones when my world is upside down, curving through space and life with just this moment to preserve in case there is no future. To have a friend somewhere in my crazy world.

I continue rolling, slowly, smoothing the clouds with my stubby delta wings. I slow roll all the way home. Would I ever see Dan Pence again? I am just a kid and none of this makes sense. Only my beautiful Skyhawk and I are together in a place where we belong; the sky. I am in LOVE all over again. Yet I am returning to the Hanna as surely as the moth to the flame. I have a knot in my gut.

FEBRUARY 1, 1970 (5)

Case joins up on me and I fly out a ways so Bullet can take his pictures. He wants some formation shots and we oblige him. Done, he radios thanks, and Case drops off my wing and crosses back under Bullet's Skyhawk to his port side. We're flying east, moving across the sky in a little v of silence.

Inordinate beauty engulfs our tiny three plane formation. The sky is pristine clear. The coast approaches washed by thin white threads. My canopy and senses soak in this green blue white whisper world. I am on the point of that pencil, thrust through the cavern of a timeless sky. It is a warm, wonderful drink from the past. With enough fuel, California is due east, straight ahead. My playmates fly silently in my view, visors down, peering into the future.

I have BDA on my kneepad. I study the circled number 15. I want it to talk to me. Have some meaning. Yet it is hardly discernible from the other things scribbled in haste around it.

I am rich. There is something to report to the Spies this mission. The part of me that is flying is ecstatic. A subdued, soft old corner of me that laughs with the girls on the bus in Sasebo, or lies in a morning bed of yellow light, it is along only for the ride.

On impulse, I yank back on the stick to pop up a thousand feet above Bullet and Turkey. I hang there briefly, then dip quickly back down. The urge to continue is powerful. Back pressure on the stick. Pop up. Roll, flick down, pause, snap up again. I become a dancing master yoyo. Bullet says nothing. Turkey watches a few moments, then begins a performance of his own. We play cat and mouse. He flies up, I slam down. We cross feet wet and begin the wide turn around Tiger

Island. No words are exchanged. Bullet watches in silvered mirrors his junior wingmen shatter rigid formality. He never utters a word, just shakes his head, gazing straight ahead to a ship and a time that await us all. Lucky for him it is a clear day and there are just two carriers to choose from. Lets pick the right one old friend, I think to myself.

When we settle down for the long fast descent to the Hanna I glance once more at my kneepad. I sense there has been a change. I feel it where I've never felt it before. I will not speak of it. Not admit it nor cry. I am here and I am here to fly and that alone is why. If I have crossed a border that is one all men must one way or another. It has come and gone and I will not think of it. Now. Maybe never. Like the wake of the ship, just leave it behind. Stash it, bury it for years. It will not touch me. I am in control of my life. A professional pilot.

Bullet leads us into the break. We flash past the bow and he breaks, followed by Turkey two seconds later. I count to two and snap into my break, pull hard and slap the gear and flaps down. Today is one of those days the ship sails effortlessly across the waves, barely dipping her bow. The horizon is razor blue. Wind of thirty knots steady down the angled deck. Perfect! At the 180 I bend it smoothly in a curve to intersect the "ball."

"Four one four ball, one point eight."

I have the ball and the angle of attack is a green donut, roll out, ease the throttle a hair, settle on the glide slope correct left for line up, squeeze more power on. Hanna belches black smoke from her stacks, but it will not affect me. I have it wired. Anticipate the sink hole just aft of the ship. Case clears the arresting gear, is across the safety line. The deck is mine. A shot of power as I come across the stern. Slam aboard; my hook grabs the three wire. The force of the trap throws me full against my shoulder harness. I've trapped. The brutal power of the catapult at the beginning balanced with force and quiet at the end of each flight. The aircraft rolls backward a foot or so, sheds the wire, as I slam the hook handle up. Thumbs up from the yellow shirt flight deck director to my right; stand on the right brake goose the throttle to get moving, get clear of the safety line quickly quickly, the Eagles are close behind, gear down, claws out, sliding down the glide slope.

Taxi up the deck. Park the aircraft, the nose bobbing as I tap the brakes. Flaps up, electrical gear off, pop the throttle back around the idle cut off detent and the engine dies behind me. Fasten the yellow restraining strap to the canopy, rising to catch the wind. The sea air rushes in. Breathe deeply. I welcome the salt and the fresh breeze. The oxygen mask dangles by one clip on my right side. It is a nuisance. A warm green thing that has left red marks on my nose and cheeks.

In the sun, warming, sweaty, somehow now very fatigued, I begin to feel human again. A human that negotiates with his feet, walks slowly and talks without a mask. That eases on sunglasses, puts both hands on the canopy rail and stretches up, out of the cockpit, swings his leg over its side to plant a flight boot on the ladder. The motion and relief and returning circulation are things I cherish. Perhaps the most contented moments I experience flying can come at the end of a beautiful flight as my arms rest across the canopy rails, the chocks are in, and there is nothing more to do except shut down, just pull the throttle back around the horn.

Today has been all that has ever been written about Naval Aviation. The aircraft performed flawlessly. The sky a reflected glory of painted hues. Mission accomplished without incident. The results will earn me a Navy Commendation Medal. Everyone in the squadron gets one no matter what, just have to pick a mission that stands out above the morass of the others.

It has been just over one hour since I released my Mark 82's. In my hands I cradle a cup of hot chocolate. On my plate is a piece of half burnt toast. Gary Case is talking. Talking about his fiancee. We are laughing, looking ahead to his wedding; that day in Fresno come Spring we'll throw him in the Holiday Inn pool and he'll marry the Maid of Cotton.

At coordinates Xray Delta 585692, someone is writhing in pain, delirious, and dying. Beside him, friends still warm, are dead.

MARCH 14, 1970

TRACEY : SEATTLE WASHINGTON

Dear Tracey, I began this letter last night, writing it in my mind. I flew a tanker hop, a welcome change from endless strike missions. The views I had sitting high over the Gulf are memories I will not trade for all the world... The moon lit Gulf of Tonkin, from Hainan, China, to the shores of North Vietnam was a vast panoply of designs. Great splotches of smoothness and textured acres of gently rolling ocean... Voices on the radio interject upon my reverie. Seabat, the Willy Fudd radar plane, tells Rampage how it is, and the formality of transmissions breaks down if for just a little while. There are long periods of quiet between the ship's cycles, while the planes are somewhere over the horizon bombing and the returned aircraft have all recovered. I fly slowly, at max endurance, floating through space in wide circles, awed by the deep set beauty of the scene before me. Tenpin came back from happy hour with the F-8's on Barcap and I gave him most of my fuel. The air was like silk, a black negligee worn by the night to beckon pilots. But this is all a game out here; give away fuel, calculate your trap weight, hope it all works out. Last night many aircraft boltered - I became concerned I had given too much away. The stars pierced my canopy as if to say, fear not. The carrier drifted in a filmy wake across the Gulf. To the west, flashes of gunfire and flares descending under parachutes were the only real reminders of the war, more than sixty miles distant. There, people were dying. Here, at altitude, it was so good to be alive. I slipped away the altitude, never moving my throttle from idle. Slid down to a nice landing, a good trap. I didn't want to go below. I wanted to stay with the wind and stars on the flight deck and be ONE with the world whispering by. So often things are breathtaking here! I try to remember the me that was flying while I'm standing on the deck. Other times I do the reverse, try to think of me standing on the deck while I'm circling the ship. They seem two separate realities - like war and peace. There is only a yearning that binds the two. There are times I am on the earth I wish desperately to fly; times when I fly I am anxious to be landed. It all seems quixotic, but I think that is how it must always be. Only one thing saves me from despair out here. This, the last line period, and the number in the cloud today was 38. It seems almost unbelievable to me. The end is near. And I have begun to allow for that reality. So often I seem only to be living an ephemeral existence, remote and detached from anything that makes sense. When you live only for the end of something, the present is left empty, bereft of honesty. I fly to fill pages in my logbook and memory. Fly carefully and professionally to survive. Into the drab and monotonous daily schedule I bring close squadron friends, music, letters to you, and dreams. I think we must all share the same feelings but confide them best to wives or beautiful blondes in Seattle. Even as I write this letter to you, I feel as though I am acting out a script, the soldier in the foxhole, sweaty, dirty, resting between fire fights, scribbling a letter to his girl in the States. There is sad but hopeful music in the background; my eyes lift up to the sky and there is a closeup of them which dissolves into the sound of incoming artillery and machine gun fire. It's touching. The whole damn thing. But when I finish this letter, I will fly event 6U, a night strike into the heart of Laos and I am not putting my arm around you, or going out to the lobby for more popcorn. I am dropping six more 500 hundred pound bombs somewhere in Southeast Asia. Little lights that go bright red and disappear in the jungle forever. The red tracers from the antiaircraft guns will spew up in thin fiery trails that slow rapidly as they climb, edging closer to me, sometimes moving with me as I dive towards them. When they fill the windscreen I am nearly paralyzed by fear. The red balls curve past my canopy, shedding a glow of sudden death by fire. The bright white flash of the exploding shells is almost enchanting — holiday fireworks meant for "me"... That was three nights ago. Tonight, it may be nothing. In this theater of the absurd, anything seems possible. There are not always happy endings. Already two pilots have been lost from the Airwing. No Ghostriders, yet. But bad things come in three's... We'll have to wait. The momentum of the cruise is carrying us to the end of the line period. I pre-flight more carefully, kick the tires once more for luck, laugh a lot more with the plane captains. The nightmare is nearly over. In Seattle is a beautiful lady waiting too and I must make it back to her. No time left for superstition, for wallowing in the past. Gotta look ahead and know its coming, a good life...Good Night Dear Tracey, LOVE and a long distance hug. Rod

MARCH 26, 1970

THEY HAVE ME BORESIGHTED

There are few days left. My senses are taut, spring loaded. I act calm and reserved, and inside I feel a light growing brighter. The number in the cloud shrinks quickly now and I enjoy popping my head in the hatch at Flight Deck Control and checking it. I can live with these numbers.

Two pilots, Griner and Buckley are not returning home. All of us are superstitious. The last day of operations has been tragic the last two cruises for squadrons on this tub. No one wants to become number three on his last damn mission.

When the final day of combat arrives, Turkey schedules me for two strikes and a spare. The last mission is a strike into South Vietnam with the Skipper. It will be a night flight, but the moon is round and full. I look forward to it. Somehow I am not threatened. It is not into Laos; it's a long way from the DMZ. If they knock me down on my last mission, I will be closer, maybe, to friendly hands. I don't expect to be shot down, or even shot at.

Skipper Vince Hagberg, "Woodpecker One," is the easiest to fly with of anyone in the squadron. He flies with complete assurance, is soft spoken, knows the airplane well and never gets rattled. The brief in Air Intelligence is light hearted, mirthful. One more time out. One more time diving into a goddamn black hole. Everything sounds the same but knowing this is the last launch makes the chatter spacey, rife with unspoken anxiety. I've been holding my breath.

The Skipper and I ride the escalator up to the flight deck leaning one hand on the black moving rail, holding our helmets and nav gear in the other. The ride is always a brief time for reflection. I glance up and down the ribbon of moving stairs. Below us, three Garfish pilots are stepping onto the escalator. Behind them, two Flying Eagles wait. A small cadre of pilots all now looking forward to one thing - the final mission. The escalator clanks and jerks, delivering us up three decks to a hatch opening on the windy wet real world. The flight deck is such a rude awakening at night!

The weather is decent. The Skipper and I head for our primary target, but at the last second, get diverted to a second further south. There is some confusion among the FAC's and difficulty in locating the right one, and then the correct target. When we finally spot the "log" burning red on the black jungle floor, the FAC clears us for our runs. We are dangerously low on fuel and the Skipper informs him we will make only one run apiece. No more.

"You're cleared in Magic Stone, east to west. Put 'em on the log, first man in. And we do have 37 in the area."

The Skipper dives into the abyss and drops his last stick of bombs. I watch them detonate in a long string. The sky lights up with flak chasing the Skipper on his pullout. Jones Beach on the Fourth of July was never so hot.

"Ok number two, you're cleared in. Move yours about 50 meters east of one's." The FAC is calm, undeterred by the guns.

"Magic two is in hot."

"Rog, tally ho," says the FAC.

I choke. If he can see me, with my lights out, 10,000 feet above him, then certainly the gunners can too. Hey, its night, I'm supposed to be invisible. My friend the Moon has betrayed me. I recoil at the thought of being blown from the sky on my last run. "You can see me

Misty?"

"Rog. Tally ho," he repeats.

I accelerate down the run in. Suddenly, lofting up directly at me — red tracers — moving slower and slower as they climb, streaking on a line stuck across my front windscreen. They have me boresighted.

I decide it doesn't matter at all where I throw my bombs. Surely no one cares anymore about six more Mark 82's. I don't. Still, pride forces me to try to drop them where he has asked.

In hot. The FAC radios, "and you've got 37 hosing you Magic Stone." Shit, I know that already. He is excited, his voice snapping, positive. I pick my target point, draw the pipper up to it. It is taking forever. Now I mash the bomb pickle. It is the last time I will hear the deep, mournful tone in my headset. It cries through my brain. I want it. I want to be out of here! There is a jerk as the bombs release; the aircraft pitches up. I pull hard on the stick... get the nose up... climbing... climbing now thank you. Straight ahead. Jink left, pull hard. I don't look back. Don't care where the bombs have hit. Slam the stick back to the right. Weaving my way back to the stars, I unload the aircraft and accelerate towards a very thin layer of cloud which offers a veil of protection. They cannot see me above it, I am certain.

The aircraft flashes through the cloud layer. Far out ahead I see the white tail light of the Skipper. I relax, breathe deeply. So long you bastards; so long War; so long Vietnam- I don't care if I ever see you again. I am FREE at last. I shout into my mask. No one hears me but it will never matter. The months of tension and the years of uncertainty, all the training, drains like old black oil out of an engine sump.

It is a special feeling to be riding high on this moonlit night, framing the Skippers A4 in my canopy, certain now I will never be a prisoner of war, the work of fighting behind me. There is relief, a beginning to believe in a future, a letting go of something deeply oppressive. I am flying in a place a generation of pilots have before me, in World War II. The last mission is the most important in life; putting miles between me and an ugly thing lurking in the recesses of violence. There, out there, that silent silver white dream called Skyhawk, pushing through a night sky diamond clear, you are my sanity, a thing of pure joy in a friendly sky. And you old Skipper, old man, old friend, sitting there silent and certain, is it the same for you?

...Lord it feels good!

MARCH 30, 1970

FATE LIES ON A LAZY SUSAN

Zack's West, our four man stateroom became the scene of the last official off the line party. We called them Extravaganzas. In a room that measured 8 feet by 8 feet I counted as many as seventeen of us crammed against the bulkheads. The tape player pounded out our favorite tunes; Peter Paul and Mary singing about going home on a jet plane; Neal Diamond and "Cracklin' Rosy." The air was foul with smoke and the smell of booze. Case returned from the Garfish party, his flight suit ripped to shreds. Across his back and butt they had used Magic Marker to write obscene graffiti. Oink, sitting crossed legged on his upper bunk, shot paper wads. He was forcibly ousted from his bunk, along with the mattress. Our party was terrific, a little out of hand, but perfect for the occasion. Asking a squadron of pilots who have just survived a war to do anything less, or feel any better was unthinkable.

The next morning, as the ship headed East to Subic Bay, still more than a day away, we assembled in the wardroom for an Air Wing briefing by two FAA reps from the States. It was a joke to all of us, telling us to be careful about midairs, talking about positive controlled airspace. What did they think we were, idiots? In the middle of the lecture, the ship's loudspeaker interrupted.

"May I have your attention please. This is the Captain speaking."

I leaned back in my chair. Nothing to be concerned about now. Was probably going to congratulate us, or maybe Warn Us about bad behavior in port, plead with us to be restrained. I listened absently, dreaming of California and a Big Mac.

"As you may already know, the Constellation (the Carrier replacing us) has locked up a screw and is having difficulty making enough wind to launch her Phantoms. Their engineering department is working hard to correct the problem and expects they will be able to make their commitment. If, however, they are unable to, then we have been assigned to relieve them on station. I am sorry to report this to you as I know you have all looked forward to the end of this cruise. But we are professionals and if we are called, then we will respond accordingly. I will keep you informed. That is all."

The chorus of groans and invective was audible everywhere on the ship. I was totally deflated. Disbelieving. Such a possibility was impossible. Unimaginable. The FAA boys said a few more words and packed up their lectern, sensing nobody was in the mood for their old saw.

The Hanna did not change direction. We pressed on for Subic Bay and we tried to go about our business as if it were all a bad dream and would never happen. In Subic, we had our Air Wing Tailhook Party, the traditional bash at the end of every cruise. They gave out landing awards and miscellaneous garbage, mostly just hooted and hollered and laughed and pressed the CAG for any news from the fleet...

It is well after midnight when I walk up the ladder to the Quarterdeck, salute and ask permission to come aboard. The Seaman on duty returns my salute, pauses, then begins, "Sir, I have been asked to inform you that the ship will be sailing at 0630 in the morning for Yankee Station."

"You're shitting me!"

"No Sir, we weigh anchor at 0630." I am completely exhausted. "Thanks." I shake my head, walk into the hangar bay and see the frenzy of activity. We have off loaded most of the ordnance and now they are frantically bringing the bombs back aboard. I stare in disbelief. It is more than I can comprehend. I turn and walk forward towards Zacks West, a deep melancholy wrapping itself around me. A tie down chain trips me — I curse it loudly. There is nothing I can do. My fate lies on a lazy susan, spun by Admirals and evil forces somewhere. I am sick of it.

The ship is barreling across the waves at top speed when I awake in the morning. We have left Subic and peace and about two hundred sailors far behind, caught unaware, stuck in Olongapo. The helo's are shuttling back and forth as is the COD aircraft, bringing the troops home.

In the Ready Room, there is a gloomy atmosphere of people wandering around, going through the motions of preparing again for war. The conversation is all obscene. They are reissuing our pistols and survival radios. It is all so dark I get up and go to the wardroom to get some late breakfast. Everywhere I go the men are saying with their eyes, "this can't be happening." The air is thick with something I have never felt before.

Turkey prepares a flight schedule. The aircraft are readied by the maintenance crews for combat, once more. It is the dull, familiar routine, and now it is done almost in silence, with deadly animation.

But there is something else. A mutinous spirit. A true mutinous spirit. Not from the Captain, or anyone in command. Yet it quivers on the lips of the crew. Several of us gather in Zacks West assessing the changing tides of fortune, the tangled web of fate drawing us back to the black hole of war. Norwood is there, along with Case and Paul Nelson.

Norwood surprises me. Mike is our nuts and bolts man, familiar with every fuze setting, every gunsight angle necessary to be the perfect bomber pilot. He knows it all, and accepts without apparent question war as duty for a career Naval Officer. But now he is angry, more than I've ever seen him.

"I will never drop another bomb. I'll put every one of 'em in the ocean. Fuck'em. I'm not going back to that goddamn war."

As he says it his eyes glaze over with a hatred born from deep within himself. I watched him closely, realizing that for the first time he was speaking from the heart about this cruise. Most of us had marched to that final day of combat with fingers crossed and unspoken hatred of what we were asked to do. We had danced around that hatred like a live bomb in our midst, afraid to do anything with it. Now it was exploding and it was almost heart warming to watch.

"How you gonna get away with that Mike? Christ, we could be out here for days! I don't see we have much choice, really" said Nelson, a terrible note of resignation in his voice. Paul was the realist, less subtle than Norwood but one who marched silently along the ordered path.

In my mind, the "experts" among the pilots, those that never seemed to complain, that filed all the required reports, that knew the weapons to perfection, were all a kind of mystery to me. They made me feel inadequate in an odd way. I could fly the airplane alright, and knew enough to deliver bombs on target, but that was merely the shadow of what I needed, if I was to be the compleat Naval Aviator. Internally, I knew I was a bust, would never make it to Lieutenant Commander. I got wobbly knees when the guns opened up on me. My secret wish to never kill anyone had been destroyed by this war. I blamed the Admirals. It left me out of step with the dance of the Vietnam war, without the words for the song we all seemed to be singing. And now my flying friends were showing true colors, spilling what was buried in the heart.

"Pablo, don't be so damn pessimistic. This whole thing is a crock and we did our part, survived the sonofabitch and there's no way they can get me to hang my ass out again. No way!" Norwood turned thought-ful after saying it. Laughed to himself. We all knew that, short of turning in our wings, we would have to do what the Admirals ordered. It was fun, though, to talk about devious methods of self protection, dumping ordnance in the Gulf, fake emergencies, keeping high and out of Laos with its Mu Gia and Ban Karai passes. There they had a hornet's nest of guns and if we could avoid them, our chances were much improved. No one seriously considered giving up his hard earned wings. We were too proud of those bloody gold badges to do that!

In the late afternoon, the Bridge requested Lt. Foster to report. He was the cryptographic officer and was busy now. The ship had slowed some, and turned to a more northerly heading. Norwood did some checking, moving around the ship like a SPY, and returned to Zacks with the latest scuttlebutt. All signs pointed to something big in the wind, but we could not be sure whether it was good or not. We plotted our course and distance to Yankee Station and a time of arrival.

Again, the Bridge requested Lt. Foster. The message traffic was furious, obviously. We sat in Zacks, drinking Coke and eating potato chips. It was hard to speculate just exactly what the meaning of all the messages was, but we wanted to believe it was good.

Yet nothing happened. It was tedious hours of frustration. Deep buried hopes lining the conversation with a light that the ticking clock seemed to be dimming slowly. I had now resigned myself to combat again in the morning. The pit in my gut was slowly going black.

At 2030 that night, the Captain, Newton Foss, clicked the loudspeaker to life and began his little speech. "May I have your attention please. This is the Captain speaking." Everything on the Hanna stopped. Five thousand men stood motionless, waiting.

In Zacks, five of us sat stiffly. We knew this was it. Old Newt' paused, drew a dramatic breath, and gave us our answer. "Officer of the Deck, RIGHT full rudder...we're goin' HOME." I lept up, screaming. We all did, pounding each other with our fists. The entire ship bounced out of the water. Norwood shook me and ran out of Zacks, hollering. Case was yelling "Shit hot" over and over. Nelson slapped the sides of his bed, "All right. alll riiight you muthers," was all he could say. A great weight had been lifted, and the Captain had done it so beautifully. There was joy in his voice, determination. He seemed as relieved and happy as the next man.

The turn of events had milked our psyches. Every man was played out, had put his heart on his sleeve and had it massaged by fate. But now there was no turning back. The number in the cloud stood mute. No one had bothered to erase it, or even wanted to. The ship danced across the water back to the Philippines.

APRIL 14, 1970

THE J-52 DIES SOFTLY

I have been sailing with the ship alone, my three roommates home already via the "magic carpet," a 707 World Airways flight. They have another cruise to make in five months. I don't.

The ship's dentist pulls two of my wisdom teeth and I live on Darvon to kill the numbing pain. Hanna has sailed the Pacific, without stopping. We pass close abeam Guam, so near I can almost throw a stone and hit the beach. Later, Hawaii and Waikiki bob on the horizon as we pause to land a few Air Force helos for a free ride to San Francisco. Mail calls are few. It is ten days of sailing, sun bathing on the flight deck, finishing up paperwork. In my stateroom room there is a narrow path between my bunk and the door. Zack's West is stacked with stereo's and cameras, pottery and dishware. It overflows into the passageway. The ship is loaded with more than four hundred crated motorcycles. We are returning, laden with gifts for ourselves.

Today they clear the flight deck and the COD's bring out the squadron pilots who flew home on the Magic Carpet. The number in the cloud is ONE. Tomorrow the ship will sail below the Golden Gate. We are two hundred miles off the coast now. Hanna circles into the wind for the recovery of the COD aircraft. When it is complete, all the aircraft that are capable of flight will launch and fly home. The Skyhawks will fly to Lemoore NAS, in the heart of the San Joaquin Valley. At least that's the plan.

Mick Cael and myself are assigned as tanker A4's. We launch first and wait for the F-8's to rendezvous. Their destination is San Diego and if Tenpin, the A3 tanker, can't pump fuel any reason, we will assist.

Tenpin tops them all off. The F-8's are fat and head out. We are not needed. The pack of A4's has launched and are half an hour ahead of us. Mick and I roll out east and head Home.

It is fantastic to be flying again. Feels good to work the rudder pedals and the hear the engine whistling at my back. The sky is rinsed clean for our arrival. A cold front has pushed east and left the air sparkling. We are anxious now. The coast will rise on the horizon, grow to real life proportions. The mountains will stretch and yawn and return to my consciousness. The coast I watched sink so long ago will return, dripping with a new reality, one I can love. I squint to catch first sight of it.

And then I see it. A thin apparition at first. In a moment, it is certain. California is resurrecting herself. I smile and smile. In my gut, it feels odd to be flying towards a coastline and feeling good. There is a twinge of uncertainty which I quickly dispel. I harbor no fears about this friendly coast.

As we cross the coastline near Big Sur, Mick pulls up the nose and tosses off a long series of joyous aileron rolls. I am instinctively doing the same. Just two words radiate across time and space between us. "Shit hot."

Two silvergray darts spin through blue California skies. Home from a war, home from uncertainty. Desperate for another life, a new chapter. Glad to be alive. We begin the long fast descent to Lemoore, throttles forward. In the distance I see the faint outline of runways and hangars. Mick leads in a wide, screaming, smooth descending arc to the break on the right runway. We fairly whistle into the break, pushing 400 knots we are the last aircraft home. He snaps right, I count two and whip the aircraft into a high "g" break. Gear down, flaps down, hook UP. Mick lands on the left side, I take the right. He is first off at the turnoff, stops and waits for me.

As I clear the runway, I unlatch the canopy, reach up and secure the restraining strap. All California is abloom. The wind carries Life past my dangling oxygen mask, into my remembered Being, and through the engine intakes. I bathe in warm, comfortable air. The nose of the Skyhawk dips gently as I tap the brakes to stay abreast Mick. He slaps the outside skin of his cockpit and beams the widest grin I have ever seen him wear. I too am ear-to-ear smiles; nodding my head to say Yeah Mick, you're right. We glide down the taxiway wingtip to wingtip, smile to smile. The war is over now, it is REALLY O—V—E—R. It is the most genuine joy I have known in a long, long time.

Into the chocks one final time in an A4. One last time to slap the throttle around the horn, listen to the turbine blades rattle and spin down behind my shoulders. The J-52 dies softly, merging into the silence of a California Spring.

There are smiling faces everywhere. My sister is there with Cupcake, a girl from Michigan. And so is Joel, a fraternity brother. They are happy to see me. I am overjoyed to see them. It has been eight and one half months since they partied in the center of the Golden Gate, threw toilet paper and waved a bright red blanket. It was so long ago, but now it doesn't matter. In the glow of the arrival, I am caught up in my old movie. The warrior returns. In a beautiful jet. Not a casket.

The parking ramp at Lemoore is wide and white and warm in the sun. I wish for a moment I could be alone. All alone. With myself and the Skyhawk. To say a proper goodbye to her. To try to understand how I have loved this experience so much yet wish never to be a part of it again. To LOVE my friends, and my enemies though I hardly know them.

The notion fades quickly. People are anxious. In the hangar are tables set with punch and cookies. Wives and girlfriends are standing with The Returned. Kids are looking at fathers they are trying to remember. Bev Norwood slips over to me and without a word, wraps me in her arms and gives me a kiss, then whispers "thanks" for helping save Mike's life. I am embarrassed. She notices, but she just smiles and walks off to find Mike again.

A poet I met once told me the title of her next book was going to be "Please don't start my Beginnings with your Endings." The hangar was full of both, running over each other in their haste to press on. I studied the scene all about me and wondered what this was for me, a beginning or an ending?

Mick walked over and answered the question. "Maggot, you sono-fabitch. Ain't it great!" He had his arm around Carolyn, better known to all of us as the Bay City Pie. He was lost in love. Just passing by, a wrinkly grin lifting his mustache for air.

On the ramp, the warbirds, greasy now, bone weary, sat quietly in the sun. All the Ghostriders had come home, borne there by Skyhawk engineering. I moved to the hangar door and gazed at this field full of jets. What a strange love affair I have had with them...whispered to them, coaxed them, nursed them down the glide slope. And killed with them.

I turn back to my other friends.

VA-164 Ghostriders 1969-70

SPRING 1971

FLYING AND LOVING AND LIVING AGAIN

My blind date in Fresno asked me about the war. What did I think of it?

I looked at her intently. I wanted to say something. but there were no words for it. I moved my eyes past her and spoke of the flying.

"Did you kill anyone?"

How incredibly naive I thought. "Oh yeah, there was one flight I got about 15 gomers, a road crew. It was pretty straight forward really."

There was a pregnant silence. She stared at her drink. When she lifted her gaze to meet mine, she asked with troubled intensity, "How did you feel about it?"

I could feel the question pierce to my heart. She was saying it was wrong. Wrong for me to be so glib, to not express even a flicker of remorse. I felt a defensive anger well up inside. "Listen," I said, raising my voice, " you can't think about it when you're doing it. Those people are shooting at you. They're killing Americans. It's you or them. I don't feel bad if that's what you're getting at. Not at all." Even as I said it I could hear the hollow ring of my words, the futility that echoed from my conscience. I snapped back at her.

"The war is stupid, but you don't have a choice. And there's no way you'll ever understand it. A coed from Fresno State just lives-in-a-different world."

"I don't see how you could do it," she said, her voice trailing off, "it's all human life." She looked back down at her drink, held it with both hands. The words stuck like an arrow, quivering in my chest.

"You just go out and do it, that's all."

She tilted her head forward to look me straight in the eye. There were tears in her eyes. I was shocked. There was no way to undo this knot, wet with tears. I was the callous, unthinking, uncaring robot. She was the tender flower beginning to open, trying to understand the world. The date was our last. When she asked me how could I have done it, I felt her shaking this thing inside me. I would not let her tears water the seedling growing there. Quietly, I buried it, again.

I did not lose sleep over it. I still liked myself. I knew I wasn't a crazy killer. True, the war had been ridiculous, everyone knew that. Like a final exam, you just want to get it behind you. The same thing with any goddamn war. Get it over with and out of your system. But it was funny how people reacted to it, especially women. Sniveling, whispering they just didn't approve. Whenever I spoke about that flight I seemed to construct a monstrous chasm between us. Sitting across a dinner table three feet apart in the beginning I was three hundred feet away whenever the conversation found its way to February 1, 1970. And it always did. Of more than a hundred combat flights it was the only one worth remembering. Most of the rest were a stinking blur. Their memories would occasionally flood into my daydreams in random attacks. But I could generally handcuff them, force them out of awareness. I was young and looking for LOVE, not bad dreams.

****

I propose to Alison, sitting in her car, parked on the Marina Green in San Francisco. In the early evening sky the Alcatraz light is blinking on schedule. The air is cool, blowing in beneath the Golden Gate. This lovely lady with blonde hair and the long Dutch last name has sauntered into my life and made it all seem so reasonable. She accepts. She has never received a letter from me, knows only that I fly to Alameda in T-28's and A-7's to see her each weekend and that I instruct others in the techniques of flying. Neither of us is willing to talk about the war. There is no tension over it, we simply never feel the need. For us, there are just the glossy-brave parts, the flying, mostly.

We spend long weekends in San Francisco where she lives. Long hikes across the city, over the Golden Gate to Sausalito. Sailing on the Bay with Joel and friends. Soaring together on Mission Ridge. Warm drives to the redwoods and Hartsook Inn. Horseback and picnics on the beaches and mountain meadows of Pt. Reyes. Every kernel of every dream I had so passionately believed in, lying on my bunk on the carrier, I began to realize. Not with Tracey, but with Alison. The flying was superb. Low levels up the coast of California and into the interior, scraping across timbered mountains and flathatting across deserts, arcing over Nevada and Pyramid Lake and breathless in the Owens Valley. I was flying and loving and living again...

My bride-to-be would understand the war, and my dead road crew. I would write it out in a letter to her someday, and with time, the memory would be healed.

Quit the Navy as soon as possible. Choose work and flying that gave me honest fulfillment. I would never let someone decide for me again, how my life should be lead. But the new dream would have to fight off the old nightmare.

The Spring of 1971 slid into May 8th. Alison and I were married in Grand Rapids. Gary and Karen Case came. For Turkey and I it was two white helmeted men-boys sure of nothing anymore, but happy to be alive and dancing on the wings of another old institution, marriage.

We all laughed and slapped each other on the back and peered into our collective futures.

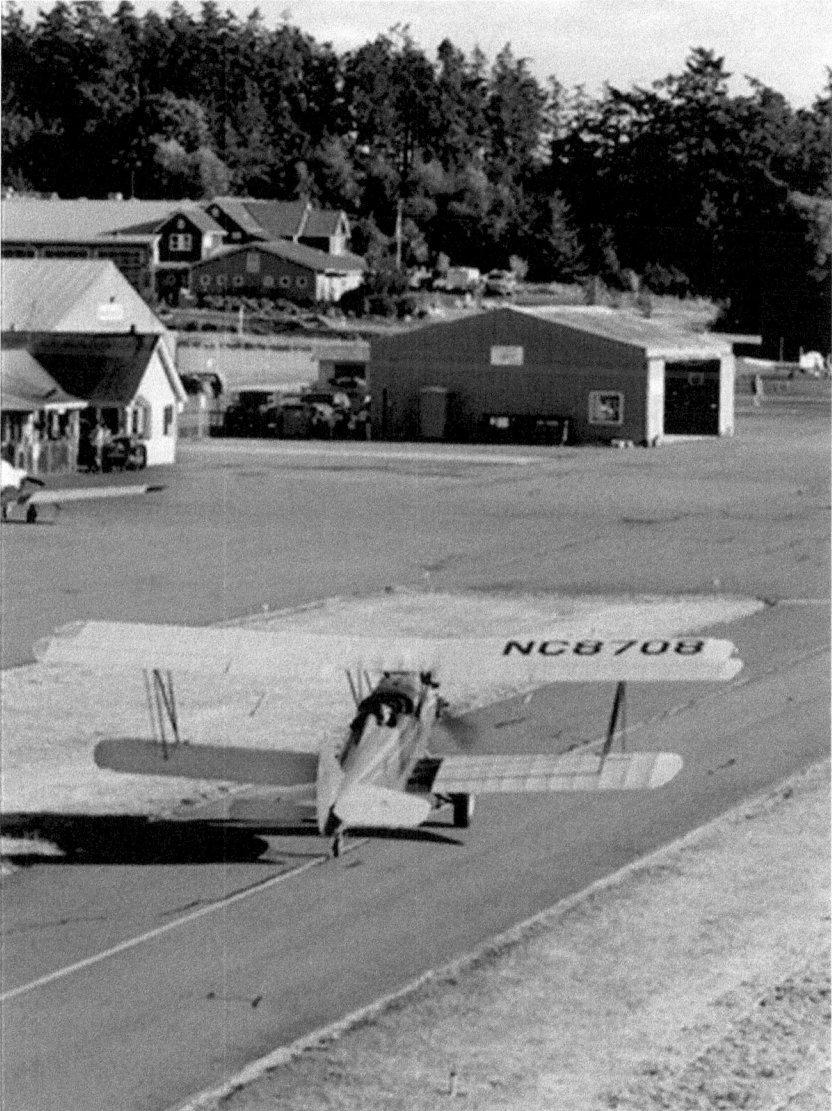

APRIL 10, 1972

FROM THE BEGINNING OF TIME

Lord, his scream was piercing. She held him nearly upside down, by his feet. The nurse stood in the far corner of the delivery room. He was red and cheesy and his face was a big frown from one corner to the other.

"He's a healthy one," said the business as usual nurse. I looked over at him from beside the bed on which his mother lay exhausted but fully aware. This moment, this brief arrangement of characters, people holding new life aloft to be examined, to be loved, to be exalted, forever etched in memory.

Arms and legs unbending, flicking randomly. The nurse hands him to me wrapped in soft white blanket. He is mine. He is not mine. He is the world's, the world is his, now. The journey has begun, with vision, with sound, with LOVE and with noise wrapped in echoes of eternity. He weighs 8 pounds, 10 ounces. He weighs nothing. He has come to us from the beginning of time. I am his guide. He is my partner. We will grow again together. We share the same birthday. Only his now seems important.

Alison reaches out to treasure this child, this life she has known better than I. Together they cradle one another in a language of movement and soft sounds, a harmony of LOVE I feel stirring from deep inside me, a thing I observe from a distant galaxy, from within me. Life constantly renewed, refreshed, uncorrupted. Whispering through the halls of evolution to this white washed hospital room. I am yours, you are mine, we are ever one. So let us begin.

I leave the University Hospital at 2AM. In the car, alone, in the dark, I feel light, am so proud. I have a son. I HAVE A SON. Dear sleeping town of Ann Arbor, WE...HAVE...A...SON! Only the street lights hear my exultation, the shouts inside our old green Plymouth Barracuda. Four blocks from home, this clear sparkling night, this first night of new life, I run out of gas. Ease the car to the side of the road, latch the doors, laughing, crying, breathing deeply. I listen to my footsteps now, I hear more than my own. The crisp air courses through me in sweet profusion. Lucky to go home this way; an internal engine guiding me, stars for companions. Will it always be thus?

OCTOBER 9, 1975

A SON A BROTHER

Moraga, California. Patiently awaiting Ryan. Born a Californian, healthy, happy. I have a videotape this time. Number Two. Alison and I have a beautiful second son, have completed our evolutionary roles, replicated ourselves, rounded out our family. He is an angel, conceived at altitude, at Lake Tahoe. Maybe there will be something unique and rarefied for him. Destiny spinning again across an interstellar landscape to land in his lap or simply flash across his field of vision. I listen to his voice in the delivery room and there are echoes again of Eternity. It is that first filling of his lungs with air and his first magnificent Hello cradled in the hands of the nurse and doctor that resonates across all time and through our hearts. That first moment we know Life has renewed itself again and we are given the chance to LOVE and be loved and live LOVE. I am so happy to be a Dad in all this, a minor role no question, yet I relish the opportunity. Yes, he may pee on me when I change his diapers sometime, he may sell lemonade on our front lawn to kids walking home from grade school, he may be a soccer goalie and a catcher in little league, wrinkle the side of our van on his first night driving. But none of that will matter. We will LOVE this son into whatever world we have brought him.

The world we ushered Ryan into IS suddenly changing. A few days later, at the supermarket I read the cover of People magazine, recognize a face and scan the article quickly standing in the checkout line. I buy the magazine, only time in my life I buy it. My path in the world changes once more. An idea bubbles through my consciousness. Around the corner from the market is the Rheem Theater, empty, unused, a movie theater with 1,023 deeply upholstered seats that rock gently back and forth. Once the finest theater west of the Mississippi. I can rent it for a day for almost nothing, $500. I make a list of the flying films I have always wanted to see on the big screen, a list of people I would like to meet and have speak at my show for that day. Some phone calls, some wild quess work about whether it will work, can I afford this or that, but a week later I have scheduled for January 1976 my very own day at the movies. I call it the Philosophy of Flight, Film Festival and Free Spirit Lectures. A lesson in overdrive. A leap off a tall building with just a cape. All this with a new born son at home. I charge only $15 for a show that will run from 10AM to 10PM. It is something only a pilot can love. I drive the whole coast of California putting up posters in airports, sending press releases to papers and flying clubs and everyone I think might have an iota of interest in my show.

Ten days before the big day. Only 200 tickets sold. I am going to lose money. I am sick.

The phone rings, someone about how to get a mention in the Datebook section of the San Francisco Chronicle. Deadline is tomorrow, do I have some pictures? I do. I race to the city. Tuesday a week later, the phone rings. Guy asks if there are any tickets left for my show? He has seen the front page of the Datebook which has not yet been published, he works at the Chronicle. I say yes, a few, with a smile.

My phone rings off the hook the weekend before the show. The day of the show, I have to turn away a hundred or more people. No standing room for this 12 hour picnic inside the theater. There are still 100 people left sitting when the last question for my featured speaker is answered at 1AM. It has been $15 for 15 hours for those hardy souls. The show has been a huge success. My cape has fluttered and my life has been unalterably changed. And so has my family's. We have all charted a new course, one that I hope has a bright future, a compass with cardinal headings glowing in the night, beckoning us to follow.

AUGUST 15. 1976

WHO WILL COMFORT THEIR CHILDREN?

Four thirty in the morning; can't sleep; sitting in front of the typewriter, fingers resting on the keys. I stare at the paper and begin slowly, a stream of consciousness pouring out.

****

The kid survived. He always did. Everyone around him smiled little snickers of disbelief. Ok to live in your own little world guy, wish I could, but you have to be a little odd to get away with it. That's what they thought, all of them. When he talked like one of them, family man, lover, swearer, football watcher, he was fine. Something slipped in though, to butter that image, make it slip out of their grasp. He had his ways and they were his alone. He loved life, but could be sad at the same time, often....

It was a gray day. You had them often at sea. Everything gray, floating on a spear to infinity. The world fled to the indistinct horizon, flying on visions of the war beyond it. The white caps were gray; the ship was gray; all that mattered was a lifeless gray except engines and animated people moving in racetrack patterns on a wooden gray flight deck. There had been Real Times, distant and full of color. They were dancing, uncaring, in deep wrinkles of my memory... The canopy closed- I was warming now, out of the steady cold wet wind that always swept the deck just before launch. I looked at the others; green suited, white helmeted men-boys like myself, setting switches: trading familiar hand signals, checking flaps: spoilers, speedbrakes. This was a ballet, prelude to a crescendo of music blasting in the center of my head; sucking heavy "g" forces with my Skyhawk above some green-foreign no man's land. Lord, I never want to set foot on it. Never! A million bombs that blew apart, scattering life, toothpicks aflame. No! Not me. I will remember this scene on the flight deck. This deep gray overcast dismal melancholy, the ghost ballet on a sea of sadness. You want color Magner? There it is. The flag. Snapping in the wind. Ripping its red and white and blue to shreds. Paint this picture. Carve it forever in your memory, Rod. When you get back home very little will remain but this gray, dull faded memory pierced only by that fluttering rag. Are you willing to die for it?... Not yet. Not yet! Goddamn I hate this war. Are we going to reenact one every generation?

Break me down, take away the chains. We are free now, the Skyhawk and I. Taxi jerk. He's signaling you to come ahead. Move it! Easy now...easy. Ok... ok.

We are gone now, catapulted in a million pounds of steam pressure and piston slamming. Flying across the gray breakers. The cat shot hurts, tickles. It releases me suddenly, swiftly: like the silence that is born shutting down a Kinner B5 engine in a pasture. I can fly now. ANYWHERE, anytime. The bird is free. Mine! Bank away from the fox corpen and climb sweetheart! Arc at seven miles, break into the clear sunshine somewhere, anywhere. Any year! Any universe...

Here we are Baby. Tally ho! Rendezvous with your leader... Its all recorded and boring and so damn formal...with mysterious war names to echo into the mike; Magic One, Nail, Rampage. Who really will ever know us or care about us years from now?

Once, the story began, I almost bought it. IFR, black night, right over my house in Beeville, Texas. Six hundred feet. Lost him. Lost the flight lead in the thick cloud. Rolled the F9 away, broke out, looking at the lights of Beeville bolted perpendicular to my windscreen. PULL IT OUT, NOW!

I survived. Shot my own approach. Survived to fly for God and country...

The kids were screaming. Fighting. My bachelor images of father-hood were a child's dream of how a Dad must be patient and thought-ful. Kids fight; but adults do it for real. Then sit down later and write about it as if it were something to change. The kids are there to re-mind me we probably never will. But they forget their anger quickly; snap back only when the urge overpowers any other sensibility. We are yet children...deep inside. Deep inside...where the hell is that? Has anyone ever seen it?

Here at 20,000 feet the cockpit is cold, and I feel it first in my toes. Always. No heater is perfect. This cocoon is tight. The eyeball dif-fusers spit flecks of ice at me. I am hot in the blazing sun but my feet are going numb! My flight suit is olive drab, the color of my Mark 82's. Am I also one, a living piece of ordnance? The thoughts dance through habit patterns of switch setting, navigating, radio chatter. Get comfortable son, the war is on...

One day, clear and blue and shiny, I killed 15 people. Nearly my rocket number in the squadron. My nickname, "Maggot," is printed on the cockpit of my airplane, side number 413. The number in the cloud changes. But the number 15 will not. Ever... I danced through the skies like a kid whose first BB shot has nailed a fleeing crow. Turkey and I celebrated on old Bullet's wings. He flew on in a fog, dreaming of his PBY, home and Flora Jean. Nothing made sense. The wardroom food was disgusting too.

I rolled in hot. A road crew. Running across the planet. "Come and get 'em boys." Which way are they runnin' I muttered. Trapped the bastards. I'll start short and walk 'em right across 'em. Go Maggot, you're in first!

We sat at dinner, spending bucks I didn't own, watching a view I did. San Francisco Bay, a light winking on Alcatraz. Beautiful lady this, sitting across from me. The body from the past with a personality so elusive, just beyond my grasp. Just that. Her voice rising. Not under-standing my candor, my apparent detachment my level emotion about the flight. I'm sorry sweetheart, but you were not there. And neither was I. It was someone else. I harbor no guilt. Can't you believe that?...Can I today?

The night was a shambles now. This conversation blasted apart by a 450 knot bomb run made years before. Made short by war stories read as a child. Heroes and patriots and glory flights. I am angry. The war was shit! I want to make love, in some beautiful, liquid, natural comforter, with Bay music crisscrossing the night around us. It will be a long drive home...

We flew a lot. Launched against our wishes and the weather and somehow screamed through the pitch nights and cavernous days to make it back. Eight and one half months. Gone. Days numbered and counted and worn like a straight jacket. I had to allow myself space to think other things; books, writing, R&R in honky Far East ports. Kids smiling, asking for money. None of it made sense. Like fishing in a barnyard. Slogging through in waders. The flying took my mind away. Far away...A broken record of war with queer names and terri-ble scratches on it. The Brief, the Mission, the flak, the target, BDA, the debrief. Gross pictures; dying for laughter. The friends I made. The close buddies I flew with and respected and shit we had to get through this together and by God we would and it helped to have nicknames and horny in port women and stupid Japanese bars and Philippine Western bands. Anything to indulge the fantasy, keep the film rolling. It was good acting to stand up in front of Life and Play with LOVE and say, "Hey, I am playing my part, here, now watch this," and tell her what she wanted to hear, to love her only while in port. I learned my role. Never violated it.

Only one thing touched reality. My stomach. It never lied. It knew. It sent wells of acid pouring into my blood when the guns were close, the night black with no horizon, the fuel low, the deck pitching, the R&R over now. I hated that. Most of all. Listen to the stomach. Intuition in chemical form. The belly barometer. But I could forget the war lying next to a woman's soft belly. There seemed to be something beautiful and enduring about that. Life was not threatened. I was living it with warmth and feeling. The combat was a puppet play. It began when the Admiral said, "All pilots, man your aircraft." He was the master puppeter. I'm sorry Sir, you can have your fucking job. Keep the carriers from running aground, the aircraft from hitting the ramp. Keep your record spotless, with countless sorties, the list as long as your bloody arm. It's your career, your war too, not mine. and its frigging mindless Are you too a puppet, Sir, like me?

I had to move over. She was sleeping now. Twisting the covers over her naked soul. Just the white of her shoulder showed and it was like a hole in the cloud cover, promising earth and home and safety. I listened to the Armed Forces Radio broadcasting the Michigan-Ohio State game. Most incredible I thought. Here, in Japan, next to a stewardess, in a bamboo tiny doll house, freezing because the heater had quit. The world never seemed less sincere than it did just then. Yet, I am free to create myth, and free to live in one...

The lightning blinds me, sears my retinas. Lord God, this is unbelievable. This storm. I can't hold on forever! We are against the wailing wall. Bashing ourselves to death. So long Ed. I am leaving you. I will find my own way through the storm. I will find my own way through Life. Free of the snarling tail of your A4. Some things I may never write about. Hints are the best I am capable of...

I looked into her eyes and said it. There was a faint smile across her lips. I felt like a book with just the bookmark showing, one she would never read. She squeezed my hand and the touch was supposed to say, "I understand." The hell she did. Nobody knows how I feel.

The game was important though, for both of us. Come, read me in the fading evening light and let's talk about things, things that matter. On this quiet, wet, rainy night, we should be able to figure out death and life and joy! Then I told her, "Listen to this music." She nodded, her eyes searching me out. She put on the headphones. I walked out into the night and froze, walking half an hour across the beach. The breakers were monotonous but full of effervescence. The rains swept inland, driving my spirit up and out with them. If I was supposed to live according to the fables, there was no time for reading on the toilet, for curling up in an easy chair with the Sunday paper, for wondering what to do... In her little room, shut away from the stars, encased in a fragile shell of LOVE, we spent the night, touching, not understanding much beyond that...

****

...I am hungry. The first light of morning is suffusing the summer sky to the east. I wrap my bathrobe tighter. Shiver some. No one is awake yet. It is early. The boys and Alison are my other world. I look at the paper in the typewriter. I have written nonstop. Now I read it and I cannot be sure it is anything. Does it even matter if it is? How many years have passed now?...Six? Yes. It seems only yesterday. How it comes flashing through my mind, anytime, anywhere, triggered by the sight of a flag, kids frolicking in a park! Anything can trip the wire that unleashes the whole cruise in an instant. A song on the radio. A tender love story on television. Anytime I see people learning to LOVE, experiencing it for themselves, I feel this knot grow tight inside me. I so want to undo it. Want to understand it. How can I put a war in a paragraph, or two? Can I erase this thing that cries to be understood, that begs me to listen? Where is the Light in this darkness?

I witness the sunrise, feel the earth slowly revolving in space...Where are the words to imprint the horrible, echoless screams of the dead on the men that would have us wage war? Who will comfort their children? I pull the last page from the typewriter and paperclip it, put it in a manila folder and hide it in my desk. It is too private.

JUNE 24, 1977

WING TO WING

Richard and I are landed in a pasture near Toulon, Illinois. My first landing off an airport. A beautiful place, surrounded by cornfields on three sides. A few feet away, a spring fed brook. The two biplanes are parked wing to wing. No civilization is visible except a red barn maybe a quarter mile away. The farmer's son rides his horse out to say hello, his dog "Fleabit" chasing along behind. Yes, it's alright to spend the night here. "Glad to have you," he says. Later they bring some hot rolls and fresh milk. Tomorrow we will press on to Ottumwa, Iowa. Tonight we will talk. And try some panbread.

Our conversation drifts across old flying experiences. Darkness melts into the pasture and our laughter. With a flashlight pointed at it, the panbread is now obviously just the right shade of brown in the frying pan. We cut it in half, and melt honey butter over it. It is thick, heavy, delicious, filling. We find more philosophy here in this cooling patch of green earth. More to laugh about...

I roll out my tarpaulin under the left wing of my Great Lakes biplane. I do not drop off to sleep for what seems hours. There is a sea of fireflies above the cornfields. Thousands of them. It seems they are dancing, a light show just for me. Tiny points of radiance rising to the stars. I wish that I could be a light in this world, even as brief as a firefly's.

The night surrounds, draws me out. I am here where I want to be, somewhere in the summer of 1977, master of my destiny now, singing with the wind in my biplane on an adventure fresh and new to me. The talk of the Navy tonight has unlocked a mental floodgate.

I am thinking about that February flight so long ago..."which way are they running?" I radioed.

I don't think it was me at all. I am not the same person. I LOVE Life. I would never murder. Nor kill a firefly. I would like to know how I came to be there February 1st so long ago, diving, pulling my pipper across the smoke and knowing my weapons would destroy Life. What part of me was KBA, what part of my life had died in the war? I wanted to ask Richard what he thought about it, how it would fit into this magnificent puzzle we call Living. It was not something I did discuss with him though. It might be like the date in Fresno, except Richard would understand far better. The question, "how could you do it?" did not have a very good or easy answer anymore. It was always simpler to brag about the flying, the beautiful things, the hazards, the close calls, the women in far flung ports.

I looked at my watch. It was almost 1AM.

I dropped off to a deep sleep. I awoke gently at 3AM, my eyes closed, ears alert. The wind was up, just a little. It was singing in the flying wires between the wings. The moisture had condensed on the top wing and was dropping in little beads to drum the lower wing just above my head. It was the softest echo of the heartbeat of nature I would ever hear. And it was a joy to discover something I had read about in books. I put my head into the warm spot on my rolled up shirt-and-pants pillow, gazing at the star filled night. Had Lindberg discovered this symphony as I did? How did such things weigh in the master plan of things? Was there something to balance the agony of war with the joy of living? I wanted to know. I was determined to fill my life with all the goodness I could and tell others that I had never found any reason to fight. Never. How could I tell that to fifteen dead souls nine thousand miles and seven years away?

I drifted back to the cornfields and my personal symphony. I felt confident someday I would find a way. Never guessing what lay in wait, I fell asleep with a troubled but clear conscience.

OCTOBER 9, 1979

IT MUST BE A SECRET BETWEEN US

In my dream I am writing a letter. The letter is furious, filled with the toxins of time..."I am talking to you February 1, 1970. Do you hear me? You have no hold on me. None. I am talking to you, my victims. I LOVE you. I LOVE you now, and I loved you then, February 1. I want to know what I did to you? Did you hear me screaming down in my dive? Did the Mark 82's whistle and shriek and were you running, running for your lives? Did you hate me? Did you know you were going to die, to be torn apart by green bombs exploding in an infinite haze of slivers?

The score was me alive, you dead. I loved you then, but I did not know it. Did you have children of your own? I do now. Did you write home yesterday, stuff the envelope in your pocket? When you were growing up didn't your father LOVE you and hold you and toss you in the air and marvel at your sweetness? Did he pray you would never go to war? I do now. For my boys, for all the Fathers and Sons and Mothers and every victim of wars we, none of us, want.

That was me, the first airplane in. Yes, and it was a beautiful day you recall. Remarkably beautiful my Friends. I know now the sunshine on my shoulder was the sunshine on yours. We should have spread out a tablecloth on the orange road, talked this over, this thing we were doing to link us forever. Had some bread, and something to wash it down. I want to know you. To touch you. I would never kill you if YOU would just touch me. Reach up slow my plane, hold me in your hands and set me gently on the road beside you. I want to shake your hand, tell you about my dreams, about growing up and flying. I have never seen a boundary line, a DMZ, from the air. They are all fictions. We are enemies. A fiction too. And I love music. Like you. So maybe we could sing together. The words would come easy. I want to know your families. Cry with you at birth. Laugh with you. Show you my snapshots. I want to feed you if you are hungry.

Did you draw stick figures too? Do you marvel at the soaring flight of the birds? Do you close your eyes and draw deep breaths among the flowers? Do you wonder where the paths of life will lead you, or where the leaders will tell you to dig, or fight?

The world is perfect. What have we done to it? Why am I here diving on you, ready to kill your dreams, take your breath away? Why have I never asked myself these simple questions before? I want to back it up, reverse the film reel. Stop. Sit down with you and talk. Smile. We do not hate each other. We hate not loving, not walking away from hate, not caring. We must make a pact, just us, the sixteen of us. We will not tell anyone. It must be a secret between us. We will not fight, ever again. If they give a war, we'll walk a different way. We'll gather in some far corner of the world, and Talk. The ships will rust, the airplanes corrode beyond repair. The bombs will sink to the bottom of the sea. We will feed each other, sing, dance, hold a circle of hands, and begin to understand. There will be no evening news. We will write long letters, send photographs.

I dropped my air medals in the trash. The kids wanted them. You see dear Friends, I am trying. I make up stories of how the world might be. Tell my children them at bedtime. Tell them how it Might Be. I cry for me now and me then. Brief tears to rinse the stain of guilt for you, for the lives you never knew. I cry too when Life is so exquisite it hurts. My prayer is not for the weary past. It is for the present, the point which commands the futures of each of us. That we forget what brought us to the orange road in the jungle. That we stop, we LOVE, we Listen. To each other.

I am out of breath... You have none. Today I will soar alone, above the clouds, silent, and weeping. At my journey, my learning, at this magnificent planet, and for the souls I made perish. I lift in thermal heat to put it all in perspective...

The dream ends. My heart is racing. I squint at the red numbers on the clock. It is 4:14 AM. Alison is curled in a ball. The dog is asleep at the foot of the bed. Misty, our cat, dreams on the chair. I go to the kitchen and pour a small glass of cold orange juice, sip it slowly and walk back down the hallway, stopping to check on the boys. I wonder where their dreams are taking them as I listen to their hushed breathing. I crawl into bed, carefully. Alison senses me, asks softly, "Something the matter?"

"No Sweetheart, just got a glass of juice."

"Ummm," she sighs, drifting back to sleep, "I LOVE you...night night."

"LOVE you too," I whisper.

I lay awake, breathing slowly. What if I could talk with those fifteen? Have I passed a relative on the streets of San Francisco? If there is a powerful force that binds the nucleus of atoms together, there must be an even more potent force that binds all humanity together...is it LOVE? And if it is, how do I LOVE the me that shattered lives so long ago - just yesterday?

The numbers on the clock flicked on, the passage of time a cruel cosmic joke. They did not speak of the year, or the day, or the experience I had lived, was living. A war has no end. I could not sleep. How would I end war I thought, my war, everyone's war?

END OF MANUSCRIPT

"The need is now for a gentler, a more tolerant people than those who won for us against the ice, the tiger, and the bear. The hand that hefted the axe, out of some old blind allegiance to the past, fondles the machine gun as lovingly. It is a habit we will have to break to survive, but the roots go very deep.".... LOREN EISELY

I DIDN'T LIKE FUNERALS ANYWAY

It was after Christmas in California, three glorious weeks of roaming around Lake Tahoe and San Francisco. The family had gathered at my sister's in Moraga and for the first time in many years, we were together at Christmas. The celebration was   wonderful. Now, back home in Richardson, Texas, after the New Year, the phone rang in my study. I walked over to it, picked it up and said "Hello" in a voice filled with bright expectation.

"Mags, Jim Painter, how are you?"

Painters voice was deep and foreboding. He had never called ME. We had talked once or twice in the last ten years. "Paints," a vice president with TWA now, had chatted about things in general, mostly just keeping in touch. We shared a mutual friend, Jim Posther, and I sensed his calling me was a grim omen.

"Susie asked me to call you Mags. She tried to reach you but couldn't." He paused, "Jim died after Christmas in Birmingham, Michigan. They drove up there to celebrate with his family. He got pretty sick after Christmas and just didn't pull out. I guess you know he was pretty bad off."

It had been two years since we had seen each other. The Fall after our trip with Scott and Katie to the lodge we left Fort Wayne for greener pastures. But we had kept in touch.

 "Well, yes, I knew he had lost weight and was taking more chemotherapy. But I didn't guess it was, well, you know, I thought about him over Christmas. Called Fort Wayne a couple times. The last time we talked was in November. It was a three hour phone call. God, we talked about everything. Spent over three hours long distance."

I stood by the phone, limp and weak. I could not believe my best friend had left this world. I felt an unspeakable loss. I wanted to dial his Fort Wayne number and hear his voice again. I wanted to be there with Susie, with their children to hold them all close. They had lost a husband and a father. I lost a great Friend. Just like that. Gone.

Painter gave me details of when the funeral service would be and described the last few days before his death. I thanked "Paints" and told him I didn't know whether I would be able to get to the funeral. When I hung up, I walked into the bedroom where Alison was watching television.

"What is it, honey?" She saw the tears in my eyes and reacted with alarm.

"Jim Posther passed away." It was hard for me to say. Very hard. Alison and I held each other and did not speak until some minutes had passed. I gave her what little information I had learned from Jim Painter and then I put on a coat. I walked down Pleasant Valley and kept walking in the evening twilight down any street that connected in the direction I wandered. I cried and I wondered if he were watching, listening. I felt he was. I told him I was so damn broke I could never fly to his funeral, but maybe I was lucky; I didn't like funerals anyway. The light Texas wind was drying the tears that rolled one by one down my face. I knew I could not travel to Fort Wayne but I resolved to mark the occasion in a personal way. Jim would understand.

Walking an hour through the winter evening, the moon once again a companion, I found myself repeating the question "what does it all mean?" over and over. When I feel this way, my chest is the center of my Being. Like a strained muscle, it constricts and seems to hold my body together. All my limbs merely dangle from it, jelly quivering at the mercy of fate. Where was the Light today? From the moon? A glow that had bathed the planet before man first set eyes upon it. Somewhere in my future, barreling down on me, were answers to my questions. But still, the most important thing was to ask the right question. It had not changed - how can I best express my LOVE?

The day of the memorial service I took my dancing Skyro-Gyro kite out to the campus nearby and in a strong wind, launched it. Flying the kite was for me, a form of celebrating life. To others, it looked like some old 'kid' working the lines of an aerobatic kite. It was my time, though, to be alone with the wind, the kite, and the memory of my friend. I thought of our long winded conversations down through the years, trying to resolve this mystery we call Life. I told him I was mad, because now he had all the answers and had left me to rummage around blasting the granite from my thinking without his able assistance.

I laughed quietly as I thought about my fascination with the "illusion of separateness." If we were not separate from one another in life, didn't it make sense that we were never separate, whether living or dead? If I was blind to the connection while alive, I could also be blind to the link beyond death. Brother I thought, this is a helluva "LOVE story," James old buddy.

The sky filled at that moment with the sound of a Continental engine moving west to east. I smiled. I looked up to discover a Bonanza climbing out from Addison Airport. It was Jim, I knew it. Yes, there were other people in the cockpit. But they were there at exactly the right moment and they did not know the symbol they were for an old pilot below, flying a purple and white kite with a one hundred foot tail. Uncanny sometimes, how the world works, in ways I have only begun to fathom.

As the Bonanza disappeared in a drifting cumulus painted across the afternoon sky, I was left with the thought that no matter how much I had learned, no matter how much I had loved, there was a great deal more of both ahead of me. Of that I was certain. Just how soon I was not prepared for.

MARCH 17, 1983

WITH ONE PERSON LOVING IT, THE WORLD IS COMPLETE

The living room looked out across the island and the bay far below. In the distance were a host of green timbered islands, jutting out of the Pacific. They lay there, inviting, slumbering among the currents that wrestled logs and seaweed up on the rocky beaches. I had come to talk with him about business. But it wasn't business we chose to talk about.

The questions flew each after the last, reaching out to hold a thought, shape an answer that was so elusive. He had just come through a nightmare of nearly four years. The road ahead was bright, the past four years a steep learning curve. Somehow he managed to surmount the difficulties, with help from a remarkable woman he married in the middle of the battle. I had struggled myself, flown precious little. Finances were chalk board squeaky. Never was there more than a few dollars in the bank, and debts though they evened off, were steep. But there was little to say about finances. They were just numbers. To be handled, cast about in computers, dredged up when the times demanded, We had something that cared little about statistics. And that was what we chose to talk about. All the thinking on the table. Ideas. What if's. What about this? This is what I believe; this is what we should do.

In the middle of the first afternoon, he asked, "What if you knew that by dying, war would end forever. Would you die for that?"

I fidgeted in my chair. I thought the question maybe unfair. Part of me said yes, most of me said no. "I don't know. I don't think so."

"I don't want to die, of course. That's a noble motive, but so many have died believing in a cause. The wars keep coming. People pick up rifles so quickly." I paused, looking up at the magnificent pine tree just off the long front porch. "It is not a question of dying. No one has to die to prove a point. It is a question of Knowing. It is that deep intuitive Knowing that tells me the world is not simply all it appears to be. That says violent deaths of innocent people are unnecessary. That death, in fact, is not what we should fear at all. Get rid of boredom, fear and anger. Work hard to learn, learn what it means to LOVE...the word is so trampled and stretched beyond meaning today."

He looked at me with a kind of knowing. He wanted to help me past my jungle deaths, a flight that had never ended. There was so much to say, to write, to do in this world. A person could not linger at max endurance forever, wasting opportunities to express his LOVE, for his family, his wife, for the planet. If there were a hundred lifetimes to live, there was still this one now to mold and shape and get on with. Like a long tether, February 1, 1970 seemed to rein me in, put blinders on my imagination, limits to my joy. I saw the world flailing on, business as usual, win-lose, you or me. I wanted no part of meaningless exercises. I had to choose a sometimes lonely path, choose friends who saw the same glory in living not colored by obnoxious, vain trivialities. I looked closely at the people around me, searching for like minded, more visionary than myself, hopeful, energetic souls.

The question of LOVE was a radiant gem of a thousand facets. It had carried me through a stack of books that spoke of LOVE in words and ideas wonderfully poetic: Ominpresence; inseparableness; quantum logic with interpenetrating universes; special relativity and synergistic ecosocial productivity; superconductivity in neuromelanin; morphogenetic fields and precession; cultural hypnosis and the implicate order; wave function versus impossible local causes; the new physics going beyond beyond, embracing every question then reaching back to things like Buddhism. I read and was quietly thrilled with each new discovery. I cast off Aristotelian logic that told me things were "either-or." I asked the question once, what if 15 dead road crew were not 15 dead road crew? Perhaps they were there in one of my futures all along, waiting for me. Maybe that is the way the world is supposed to work, I thought. Still, I could have chosen a different future, one without Mark 82's, without 123 combat missions and dead lifeless "enemy" in it. If I could speed up time, and be there where all my futures ended, I could select one that mirrored LOVE perfectly.

"I asked myself once, very seriously, what would I do different to end wars if I had, say, ten million dollars at my disposal." I leaned back in my chair and crossed my fingers behind my head. "I found it wasn't a simple thing at all. It was easy to get discouraged no matter how beautiful an idea seemed."

"What kinds of things did you come up with?" he asked with a wry smile. He liked to hear crazy ideas because nothing was really crazy to him, just different.

"I decided there would never be a nuclear war. That was a kind of calm little decision for me. I didn't want to agonize over it... It was another form of fear, disguised as an adult problem. And you know what they say, that what we resist in our lives will persist. To discard the idea of nuclear war, I would first need to replace it with something else which accomplished the fact. I did not need money to do that at all."

"And you replaced it with what?" he asked, his eyes very intent.

I had stumbled across a thought in the book, A Course in Miracles, "Peace is impossible,", it said, "to those who look on war. Peace is inevitable to those who offer peace." I pondered that for a long time when I first read it because it stirred something deep inside me. I was living with the war more than I realized. In dreams, or just driving down a road sometimes, tears welled in my eyes remembering the people I had murdered from the sky. I was focused backward in life when I did that, snagged on a limb of time and clinging to it. I had to let it go, let the war go away, brush it off and look at peace.

"I decided to offer Peace," I said, "to find ways to do that, methods and means and I wasn't sure just whats. Not very original I guess, but I figure I am being led that way so I might was well get on with it."

"And what were the changes that took place?" He smiled broadly as he asked.

"I have a manuscript at home," I said, "that I haven't finished. The last line asks the question, 'how would I end war, my war, everyone's war?I want to finish the thing. Get beyond it. Answer that question. I don't have to die to do it. I don't need ten million dollars. All I have to do is learn to LOVE. To let myself be healed. Where one person is Loved, the world is working. With one person loving it, the world is complete."

"Kind of a tall order isn't it," he mused. Behind him, beyond the tall windows on the south wall of the house, the wind was picking up. The pine trees swayed in a rhythm and grace that focused me hypnotically in the future. But images of the past flooded in. Jim standing on the bank of the Au Sable. Norwood smiling on the revetment at Danang. Now dead too. Spun in. Lost at sea in the Gulf of Mexico. Mick Cael asking me, "Where you been, Maggot?"'

"Yeah, it's not easy," I answered. The moon would be full tonight. It was rising behind the pines as bright as a silver dollar. "But I think most pilots would trade their combat experiences for a world advanced enough to be at Peace. Soldiers that stuck bayonets in the guts of men whose eyes they could see share that dream."

"We are all actors," he began, "on a bright stage surrounded by music. There is no orchestra and there is no curtain to fall. WE are the audience, the drama-script, the bit players. All weapons are marshmallows that can never harm the real Us. But as we believe we can be hurt by the characters invented for the Play. Smashed by the weapons we hurl at one another, by that measure have we forgotten how to LOVE."

"And how to laugh," I added quickly. "Remember the time we decided all bombs should be filled with flowers. I'll never forget our ultimate weapon, the 'atomic bloom.' I haven't laughed so hard in years."

When was I happiest I thought? Always when I discovered myself smiling or laughing. Maybe viewing Charles Kurault; listening to Garrison Keillor on public radio give the news from Lake Woebegon; or watching the children wheel off to school on their bikes. There was a kind of glow within that could not be dimmed by the evening news no matter how violent it was.

The evening merged with the warmth from the wood burning stove and mugs of hot chocolate. The moon rose high above the island mountain playing hide and seek with low scudding clouds. I thought of Jim again, felt him nearby. And I asked myself, quietly as usual, how can I best express my LOVE?

In bed that night a fierce storm ravaged the island, knocking out the power. In the wind and rain and thrashing pine boughs slamming against the house, I felt a very powerful presence. Sleep did not come early. I lay there in a twilight zone of swirling questions and faces of friends come down through the sky to visit. In the middle of a thought I saw my fifteen enemy-friends gathering round me, not somber, not smiling, simply there. And they were whole. In the far corner of the room was a familiar face, a lady I knew but could not place. I spoke first.

"Hi," I said to them all, "finally we meet." I was afraid to open up. If this was a lucid dream, I wanted to remember it. I would move slowly.

"We are here to offer you Peace, Rod. It has been a long the time for you, struggling in supermarket lines, asking the question 'how could I do it? again and again to the mists around you."

Listening was all I had to do. I saw them warm and whole human beings just as I knew they must be. My old dream was right; they loved their children and filled their lives with laughter and tears. There were distant echoes of explosions; thunder bouncing off island peaks in the storm. I am, I thought, in that space where total Consciousness exists, where every answer is without a question. I was dancing in eternity.

In the corner of the room, the light grew brighter and this Radiant Person walked toward me, slowly, smiling. I wanted to reach out and touch this creature, knowing that when I did my life would begin anew. A bolt of blue white lightning ripped through the night and once again the bed was soft and I was thirsty and there was the storm outside and my enemy-friends were gone. I rolled my head on the pillow to watch the magnificent pyrotechnics out the big window...in the morning I would have some news for my hosts. I drifted off to sleep and waited for the sunrise.

The conversation spanned two full days. We did manage to talk some business, but I left the island like a corked bottle with a new message. I floated on a sea of timelessness and the scribbling on the note inside me, for whomever cared to read it, said this: "Sailed for the other shore this day. Expect to reach it soon."

****

"...It is perspective that shows the barriers between men to be imaginary things, made real by our own believing that barriers exist, by our own believing that barriers exist, by our own bowing and cringing and constant fear of their power to   limit us." ..... RICHARD BACH

LOW LEVEL AROUND HAWAII

SUMMER 1984
THERE ARE NO STRAY BULLETS IN THE UNIVERSE

My lips were beginning to chap from the hours of wind and sun in the open cockpit of the 1929 Fleet biplane. Be there sometime next week I had said. "There" was far off Oregon. "Here" was Texas, the panhandle, a day's flight at one thousand feet in fierce headwinds. Ahead of me on the horizon were the chalk white silos growing in the heart of Dalhart. Like a weed on the prairie, they stood stark against the clean line where sky met land. The biplane barely inched west in this wind, bouncing with every turbulent thermal and gust that played in the summer air. I would refuel in Dalhart, and press on.

There was no traffic at the airport. I had no radio, just my eyes. And they swept around the pattern easily. There was the windsock, straight out, forty five degrees to every runway, favoring if any, the runway dead on my nose. Just ease the throttle a hair, wait for the Ole Fahlin propeller to drag itself round to a kinetic flickering, the Kinner radial popping mufferless in my ears and to the wild creatures on the ground who might remember that sound of a different day. If indeed time is just our invention, what a marvelous gift the sound of the Kinner of an evening in 1929 brought alive in 1984. The Fleet settles on her black main tires, tail up in this wind, the stick laid into it. I have her in full control - my feet dance on the rudder now left now right, easy sweetheart, that's right, keep her straight and we are down, turning at the first turnoff before the tumbleweeds sweeping across the taxiway. Ah, Dalhart, your messengers from the prairie sent to welcome me - thank you.

At the gas shack, the screen door swung open and shut with the wind, slapping its faded gray white pine boards like the one on the front porch of my Dad's home farm in Minnesota. It had always slammed shut, no matter what. Sounding a bit like a dead snare drum when it did. The flies always found ways through it and maybe it was the beating of their wings that made that tinny sound. I had fond memories of the old farmhouse, but it had burned last winter, burned clear to the ground. Here there were hardly any flies. The heat kept them in the shade, or the smell of the avgas stewed their brains, whichever. I was looking for a cool drink, and some 80 octane for the Fleet. Inside, it was as hot as the tarmac, and near as dark.

No one was home. Just a sign propped up on the counter. "For Gas, call city hall." Below it was the number, and an arrow pointing to a corner of the room. The phone was there, hanging on the peeling wall like a melting chunk of black licorice, chipped and ancient but still familiar. Thank God it wasn't a pay phone.

I wondered who I would ask for at city hall, the mayor? The dial labored as it spun around slowly, ticking off the numbers I read from the sign across the room. I loved this kind of place. Efficient, I thought. No hurry. No war to get to. No mission to accomplish. But damn, it was hot. I was thirsty and the water cooler was outside, looking rusted and forlorn. Not much hope from it I decided. Would have to be a Coke from the machine.

She answered at City Hall. A sweet, west Texas accent dripping across the phone lines to spill onto the floor of the Line Shack. "Hi, I'm out here at the airport," I said, "just landed, wondered if I might get a little 80 octane?

"Yes you might," she said cheerily, "might be a few minutes though, if that's ok with you. I have a letter to finish typing, need to get it posted before the post office closes. Can you wait maybe 15 minutes?"

"If I can work the Coke machine, you got a deal!"

"Sometimes it gets a little stuck. A good kick on the left side usually cures it. Be there in a few minutes." She was so pleasant and so sure I began to look forward to our meeting. But first I had to have a Coke.

The machine was not a problem. The coke was in an old bottle, probably used by three or four thousand people in the span of its lifetime.
A small bottle, the one that fits snug in your palm. But the price was
1984 vintage and the fluid was cold. It bit into my lips and bubbled
on my tongue and I remembered on the carrier after every flight, I
had to have a frothy Coke, poured over a tall glass of ice. I gave up
Coke after the cruise, knowing I was hooked on the caffeine. But today it was as if I had never quit. Must be what an alcoholic feels after
years on the wagon. I stood there, looking first at the bottle in my
hand, then through the screen door to where the red and yellow Fleet
stood beside the gas pump. How far from that time I was where
the Pacific filled my horizons. Here it was summer heat on a deso-
late prairie, with an aircraft that cruised at a speed barely enough to
move the slats on my old Skyhawk. And wasn't it odd, I thought, how
things triggered old memories, like the Coke and the screen door.
Memories of good and bad, points in time where this future moment
would have seemed beyond even a dream.

I had some time, time to read the bulletin board. There was an FAA
notice about traffic patterns in the area, and some low level training
routes not far off. It was dated six years ago. Nothing happens fast
here. Somebody's Aeronca was for sale, but the picture had fallen off
the 3x5 card and just a spot of old glue remained where it had been.
There was a T-6 for sale over in the next state. Then there, and I
laughed when I saw it, with a quick sudden cry of recognition, was a
cloud with a number in it. The number was 241. Below it on the 8x11
paper was an ad for aircraft insurance from a Dalhart broker. The
number made no sense until I read the small copy at the bottom. It
was the number of aircraft he insured in the tri state area. I figured
it was some kind of record. It was almost the number I had
written once in a note to myself just after the cruise started, sitting in
flight deck control feeling as though my days were a thousand pound
weight. Today the number in the cloud was a sad joke. Maybe it always should have been. And I wondered where the artist was now
who drew the grease pencil painting of the Golden Gate on that plex-

iglass. I tilted the Coke bottle up for another long swallow and turned to face the door.

Heat rising from the runways wobbled the picture of Texas yawning from every point of the compass. The Fleet seemed to be undulating waves of color floating above a silver mirage. I loved moments like this, alone with my destiny, that little biplane out there, and the dust and the heat and sweaty forehead. Mother Earth broiling us together, flavoring the hours with a timeless kind of LOVE. I could hear my breath moving in and out, felt ripe and perfectly a part of all that has ever been. Knew without feeling strange I was a tendril of life reaching out to know itself. I gulped another lug of my Coke and watched and waited, standing alone before the screen door. Events already cast in time were waiting patiently all around me. I smiled and said "hello," believing in their perfection.

I saw the dust rising in a line, moving towards me, long before the dot of a car could be made out. The wind kicked the cloud into a brown haze, a trail in a bubble chamber, an electron headed for a collision. Headed for me I was sure, the voice on the phone and our little rendezvous with destiny. To fill the 27 gallon tank in the top wing of the Fleet. How sublimely wonderful were the machinations of fate. I waited expectantly.

She wheeled her yellow Camaro across the ramp and parked beside the gas shack. Getting out of the car, she paused to study the Fleet. It was unusual to see a Fleet, something so old so pretty, so well preserved, still flying. It was a gift for those that cared enough. It gave me a moment to look at her before she would be too close for that kind of scrutiny.

Cinnamon brown hair wind blown and medium length. Eyes dark, wide and alert. White blouse loose fitting tucked into a narrow waist. Levis blue white from wear, white running shoes. Pretty new. Red finger nails. A touch of lipstick, red to match the nails. Always for me there is a brief flash of intuitive matching, curves and form laid on an internal graphic of a perfect companion. In the first instant is laid the first translucent layer of many which begins to animate my mind and the words which tumble from it. The way she speaks, the way she moves, each succeeding event will reinforce the preceding until something comes along to shatter the image animating, building in the studio of my mind.

She bounds up the steps and flings open the screen door.

"Howdy," she says, a toothy white smile framed between soft cheeks. "Reckon you are my gas customer for the day - sorry I took so long."

"That's alright, no problem. I needed a little break from my time machine out there."

"It sure is a pretty thing. It's a Fleet isn't it? What year?"

"Yep, it's a 1929 Fleet...How is it you know a Fleet when you see one, are there more around here?"

"Oh, I guess I've seen a couple. Once you've seen one, you remember them easily. There aren't any real close by here. One in Clovis, New Mexico and one up towards Wichita that comes through here on his way west. None as pretty as yours though. I suppose your flying west too. I didn't hear you come over town so I figure you came out of the east, right?"

I laughed. Here was an intelligent woman. And she knew east from west, though I reckoned maybe here in west Texas that was necessary for survival. "Just about. Out of the south east. Left Dallas early this morning."

"My name is Carol, Carol Martin. Nice to meet ya..." She reaches out a hand to shake.

I am still processing this bit of prairie flower before me. Something warm and revealing has entered this space, made me forget entirely the heat and dust. When it happens, I feel like a kid, a little foolish, a little befuddled. Instinct preens my ego, my thumbs straighten the sweat soaked shirt around my waist and I wipe the sweat from my brow. My hand meets hers reflexively and my conversation flips to autopilot. "Helloo...I"m Rod Magner." I can hardly say my name. There is a catch in my voice. I don't even know who has said it, me or a ghost wave of me. I want to be her equal, but I feel I am in the light of a cosmic orb. I won't look at her this way I say to myself, then I'll be ok.

"Welcome to Dalhart Mr. Magner, where the panhandle meets eighty octane, right? Not many still burn it, but we keep it for nice planes like yours. Here's the key for the lock, handle's on the side and ladder over on that side of the shack, be out to help you in just a sec." She hands the key to me and moves around behind the counter. "Thanks Carol." I spin and move out the door, down the steps and around the corner of the shack to get the ladder. What in the world is a woman like that doing in Dalhart, Texas, I wonder? My thoughts, a few minutes ago so sure of control are coming unglued. Maybe she is a stream of high energy particles aimed at the likes of me. This is an atomic event, right here in the middle of a cyclotron called panhandle, Dalhart, Texas. Ten minutes ago I was looking at my watch, figuring the daylight left, the distance to Raton, New Mexico where I intended to spend the night. There was adequate light left certainly, but maybe it made sense to not press it. Already I was eight hours in the cockpit, enough for any day. Especially a hot one. Funny how all the figuring was colored by this lovely woman driven into my consciousness in a bright yellow Camaro. I shook my head, picked up the ladder and walked over to gas the Fleet.

Carol came out and steadied the ladder in the wind as I leaned over, watching the red avgas carefully. I wanted to fill the tank completely, without spilling any in the front cockpit. She wasn't wearing a ring, a good sign. People seem free to talk without rings...no relationships to defend.

"I had planned on making it to Raton tonight. This wind though, I don't know."

"Raton's a hundred thirty nautical from here. That's about what, one plus forty five no wind," she said. "You might be watching the head-lights at the drive-in trying to get'em to start the show when you get there."

Uncanny I thought. She knows this planet like the palm of her hand. Knows even the average cruise speed of my Fleet. If she gives me half an opening I thought, its Dalhart tonight, Raton tomorrow morn-ing. Period. And I knew as I said it I was going nowhere. I had just shaken hands with an alternate future and it had things to tell me.

"Yeah, could be a little tight I guess." The thought lingered like late morning dew in the shade of a tree. Maybe I can save a little fuel to-morrow too if this wind dies down. No sense fighting the tug of fate here holding up my ladder. I put the big red gas cap on the tank, snugged it down good. Climbing down the ladder I said to her, "Car-ol, I think you've made my decision for me. An early start tomorrow and Raton will be easy. Might make Cheyenne by nightfall if I'm off at first light. Nice time to fly too."

"Good!" she said, sounding sincere. "Always nice to have vagabond biplane pilots add to the local economy." The way she said it I felt welcome. Genuinely excited. Anxious for the evening to unfold.

We rolled the Fleet away from the gas pumps and across the ramp to a tie down. I tied the tail and a wing, she did an expert job on the other wing. I watched her from the corner of my eye. Everything about her was remarkable. Her efficiency was obvious in everything, from her dress, her makeup, her words, her hands in motion looping the tie down knot just so.

My garment bag was an old black heavy vinyl thing the parariggers had sewn for me in the Navy. It carried a ton of whatever I wanted and was strong enough to withstand hydraulic fluid and heat in the hell hole of an A4 where I stashed it, just under the tailpipe. It had flown cross country in A4's and A7's, and I wondered what it thought of being rolled up in the front cockpit of a Fleet after such high times. Probably like I did - slower, but able to stop and smell the roses. It happened often in an open cockpit airplane. The scent of the land was everywhere in the cockpit. I liked it better, even though I was not rolling inverted or pulling high g's. There were compensations for windy high drag flying. Dalhart Texas was one. No Skyhawk could land here and call city hall for fuel. I hefted the bag out of the cockpit, set it on the ground and buttoned up both cockpits after Carol was finished peering into them. She liked the smell of an old airplane she said. The fabric and wood and rocker arm grease, it was all a kind of perfume you couldn't wear but you wanted to be around. How did this woman know all that, say it so perfectly I asked myself?

"You must be a pilot Carol. Only a pilot says those kinds of things."

"I was a stewardess once. Did a lot of flying of a different sort then. But then I became a nurse. I've had some flying lessons, soloed a few years ago. But I don't have many hours. Just like old planes better than the new ones...You said you were headed to Oregon, you've got some flying ahead of you!" She said it with a note of awe in her voice. I remembered what it was like when I gassed planes in Ann Arbor. People passing through on flying adventures. I wanted to be like them, flying off over horizons, looking down at the planet, enjoying the scenery. She had that air too. Sad I thought, stuck here in Dalhart, she must be yearning for her freedom. "Well, you've seen some of the world then beyond those grain elevators over there. I'd like to know what brought you here to Dalhart, but first tell me where the closest clean shower and bed are."

"Sure," she said, "only one place to stay, the Panhandle Inn out on highway 54. I can take you there, no charge since you bought all that gas." She smiled, turned and strode briskly into the gas shack. I followed her, setting the ladder around the side where I found it before I stepped up into the shack.

"Cash or plastic?" she said, her chin up, eyes focused directly into mine.

"How about plastic?" I said.

"Plastic it is." She pulled the little receipt folder out and laid one in the imprint machine. I signed, she gave me the receipt and that was it. I stepped outside, picked up the black garment bag baking in the sun and she opened the trunk for me. The next moment we were aimed at downtown Dalhart, dust flying behind us, a yellow Camaro full of questions.

"Carol, I feel as though I've met you before," I said. It was something I had said many times to women, but rarely meant. This time was different. "I feel like I already know you, that our paths have crossed somewhere before."

"This planet's not so big that that's not possible," she said. "In fact, its very likely."

"What airline did you fly for?"

"Pan American."

"Well, I've never flown Pan American, so I wasn't a hungry passenger ringing the stewardess call button. Must have been somewhere else." She didn't say anything for a few moments. She appeared to be collecting her thoughts, though I had already decided they were well organized inside her beautiful head. I gazed out at the panhandle landscape brushing past my open window. The land was a stubble beard, sagebrush speckling its face in little pockets of life. The velocity of a wave, I recalled, can be determined by multiplying the wavelength by the frequency. This wave I rode was pulsing in high frequency. I sensed we were on a wavelength that was years in amplitude, that moved with precision through all space-time. If I had wanted to disembark right then, I could not. I had shaken hands with this future and it was alive, and very special. The velocity of this wave was superluminal. Wherever it was carrying me, I was already there.

I spoke boldly. "Carol, could I take you to dinner, after I've cleaned up? I would really enjoy talking with you." So often I felt that way with people. Just wanted to toss ideas out, talk about things that mattered. So few really wanted to, for whatever reasons; jealous husbands, no time, or more pressing interests. Caught up in the maelstrom of day to day decisions, there was never any space to paint a brighter picture, to play with crazy questions. Most of a conversation was spent defending the ego. I would listen as eagerly to a new physicist as I would to Carol, but in Dalhart I wanted to talk with her and the chemistry seemed right. Besides, she loved old planes and the smell of rocker arm grease. Her intellect was clearly in the right place.

"I'd like that very much," she quickly responded. "We'll get you checked in at the Panhandle first. There is a nice casual restaurant if you like Mexican food just out of town on the highway. Sound ok?"

"Sounds perfect," I said. "Give me an hour. Guess you'll have to drive again."

"Fine with me."

Lord, the way she talks, this happens every day. Pilots come to the airport, see her, fall in love, and she gets a free dinner. But there was something in that thought which didn't ring true with me. I couldn't put my finger on it, but I knew it was something she had said, maybe the way she had put it. This was not her normal operating mode, she just made it seem simple. I accepted it for the moment, let her drop me off at the Panhandle Inn, a kind of adobe looking place set back off the road a hundred feet. The rooms were large and old, clean but with an odor from years of bodies passing through that Lysol and pine scents could not erase. It seemed entirely appropriate to the landscape which was barren and plain but for the low buildings, power lines, single railroad tracks, and parched grain elevators. Who in the world did a Carol Martin find to LOVE her in this place I wondered?

I showered and tried to unwrinkle a yellow pullover shirt to wear with a pair of sta-prest Levi's along for the trip. I had a pair of deck shoes I called my dress-ups, which I brought only because Alison had insisted I have something nice besides my Nike's. I prefer to travel light, have few options in dress. That way I can keep away from formality and be myself. I haven't worn a necktie for months, maybe years. It drives Alison nuts. But I used to watch men whose duty it was to wear them and they quickly loosened them on the drive home. If something bothers us like that all day, why must we put up with it I thought ? It was another example of the little hypocrisies we live with that somehow lead to bigger ones which for me ended up 9,000 miles from home dropping bombs on jungle roads with people running on them.

I looked out the window of my room and up at the evening sky fading to red-orange. One of my futures was flying overhead, leaving a contrail on its way north to Denver. An airliner, maybe a Southwest 737 which once I had expected to fly, was making headway against the jet stream. I knew what it looked like from the left seat of his cockpit. I had my type rating in the 737, but had never used it to earn a living. A part of me always paused to note the passing of that alternate future, while another aspect said, maybe you're better off my friend; there may be more to life than hauling passengers through controlled airspace.

The yellow Camaro arrived right on time. In it was a new lady, one dressed for dinner with a simple print dress. I had never seen an aura around anyone, but there was one tonight. I couldn't see it as much as I felt it. And Carol had the scent of a California mountain in Spring...I was popping the canopy on my A4, latching the lanyard and breathing in the Spring air of my arrival at Lemoore fifteen years earlier. Taxiing next to Mick, the war finally over. It was yesterday, it was now. Fresh as the wind that blew across Texas tonight, a memory never lost to time.

"Hi Carol. Is this the Yellow Cab of Dalhart come to fetch hungry air travelers to mysterious Mexican haunts?" I said it kiddingly, but it took too long, sounded too preplanned which it really wasn't. I was plainly nervous.

"No, this is the Carol Martin of the daytime going to the Royal Ball in her yellow pumpkin with the Prince of the Airways." She smiled as she said it, putting me completely at ease. "Would you be him?"

"Does a bear sleep in the woods?" I rejoined.

"Does a Prince sleep in the woods?" she laughed. "And would you care to drive, Mr. Airways?"

"If you trust my driving this chariot, you are most certainly a perceptive woman." It would be fun to be in command of the Camaro, to wheel down the main drag of Dalhart like a long time resident. I was beginning to feel the evening wrap around me like an Indian blanket. In this corner of Texas the stars would be bright away from the lights of town. I was suddenly quite hungry and Mexican food sounded good. We drove west 2 miles, past the city limits, out highway 54, to Pepe's.

Pepe's was not crowded. We took a table near the back, a spot where I felt comfortable, thinking it would be more private and we might be freer to speak. The menu was already on the table, wedged between the metal handles of the salt and pepper holders. Good restaurants, I think, put their menu's where you can get them right off. They usually have formica tables too, like Pepe's. And plastic placemats with pictures of Mexico, thumbtacked to the walls. I wasn't concerned about spending much for dinner here, even without looking at the menu. Carol said "Hi" to everyone in the place. For a brief second I had the feeling again of being taken, another sucker pilot on the arm of a pretty town single. She was careful to reassure with a smile that said she knew I had thought that and not to worry.

The water came, icy and dripping down the sides of the tall glasses. As I lifted it to toast the evening deja vu struck. I had been here before, with her. I reached into memory --- tried to hold it, draw it out, see where it was leading. But it drifted off. Why did that always happen? Once in Vietnam it happened in the middle of a bomb run. Through all that intense concentration, came blasting this sudden image; I was going through the motions, had been here before. I looked at Carol and told her.

"Well Mr. Magner-"

"Please call me Rod," I said, "or Mr. Airways if you wish."

"Rod... I believe in deja vu. I even believe we've met somewhere. When you fly, time is altered and nothing is ordinary about life anymore. So I'm never surprised. What did we order back then?"

"Whatever it was it probably has spoiled by now. We should try something different, and that might change the future. Besides, I don't remember." We both chuckled at our cosmic humor. And we ordered the same thing.

We talked about Dalhart, the seasons that split the sky here into tornado alley one month Sahara heat the next. Small talk, a kind of breeding ground for the next generation of contact, necessary for every conversation, consumed the first water glass. I leaned back in my chair, listening to her, finding questions I would ask, studying her eyes. The conversation was simply an excuse to keep my eyes on her then.

"Do you believe in chance?" I said.

"No."

"Why not?" I asked.

"There are no stray bullets in the Universe," she said, pausing for my response. I thought of the red tracers drifting up at me in the night, scaring me silly. Each one aimed, intended for me. Must be prairie philosophy she is endowed with I thought. But maybe she's right.

"Then it's ok for us to be at Pepe's tonight, or any night, and whenever we are, it's not chance. I guess I agree," I said, smiling. "And this conversation has meaning beyond this hot evening."

"If we wish it, that's right," she said.

We began to talk about flying, how we had come to it, what it had meant in our lives. The first attraction was a little bit of glamour, then came a feeling of accomplishment, membership in an elite fraternity, a sense of power, mastering of nature. Rolling inverted at 30,000 feet had always been my way of saying I was in control. Then one day, after completing a test flight in an A7 high over the San Joaquin, I stopped to survey the planet below me. California stretched out in a curving away hologram, the Pacific framing the west, the Sierra's and Nevada the east. San Francisco was barely visible far to the north. It was remarkably intense, the color, the timeless grandeur, all focused for a shining moment in my heart. I said to myself, Lord, if I could just once show this to every person on earth, what a difference it would make. In that brief instant of my life my mission was infinitely clear. There was room for every one on the planet, acres of room. You down there, crawling on the freeway to work, cramped with worry and frustration, angry or bored with living, come up here alone some time and see for yourself. I would gladly share this with you.

I told Carol about that day. And then I began to tell her about February 1, 1970. Here was a stranger who might understand. I told her that day had balanced my scale, kept a pointer motionless in my life. I had searched for guilt, tried to find it. Cried silently when I thought of the fifteen lives wasted by my bombs.

I went on, "But instead of finding guilt, what I found more often was pure ignorance. I was naive, my victims we're stupid. We should not have been there in the first place. What did we expect from hurling bombs and gunfire at one another? Still, I wanted to feel guilty. Yet I only felt guilty because I didn't feel guilty. A false guilt if there ever was."

Carol was listening with the softness of a goose down pillow. My words seemed to find an ear linked with the Universe. I thought of Jim telling me that we needed stories to remind us how precious each of us was. That the illusion of separateness was only that, an illusion that did not bear up in the full light of LOVE.

"And you have learned that enemies are but friends in the shadows of LOVE. They are an indestructible spirit. That Friends are somehow always with you."

"Carol." I shook my head trying to shake loose the words I needed. "I once felt that to ask the best question would guarantee answers that would keep nations from going to War. Keep kids from enlisting to die or to kill. Our animal instincts may show us what we were, but they do not begin to tell us what we ARE. If instinct is all there is to LOVE, just animal urges, then we are doomed to repeat our cycles of violence."

"I don't think you were mistaken Rod. The right question IS very simple...How can I best express my LOVE? As the answers come and go, your life will grow and change. As you express your imagination more perfectly, will the world perfect itself."

Carol had not taken her eyes off me. She paused before speaking again.

"I worked emergency and saw terrible things. Night after night. I was also in pediatrics, in the delivery room." She stopped, looking past me, remembering something in her life that affected her deeply. She told me then about premature babies born tiny enough to hold in her palm. Alive, a quivering mass of humanity; she could feel the heart pulsing, racing against time, struggling, its life held by the merest of threads. And the doctors knew there was no hope. They ordered her to "put it in the bucket" and then they told the mother it was stillborn. A lie. A compassionate lie perhaps. "But I had to put the baby in the bucket. They wouldn't do it." It was like drowning little kittens, except they were tiny human beings instead. She quit talking, her eyes misty and far off.

"But there were normal births too," I added, "that seemed to balance the pain?" I said it hoping to lift her heart maybe an inch. Selfishly thinking I might also lighten the scales of my own dilemma as well. She didn't seem to hear me.

"And wars," she began, "drive wedges where they don't belong. My father only recently confided a story from World War II, a horror of death for a ship load of men, a friend among them, bodies stacked on the deck as they were pulled from the Channel. As he told me, tears came to his eyes - I had never seen him cry. Had never felt so close to him, and now I think maybe that was one of the reasons. All I could do was hug him."

She reached out as she spoke, touching my arm now and again, just ever so lightly. Here was a woman who had seen more of life in the trenches than I ever would. When she touched me, the warmth of her being curled up inside me. I wanted to offer my hand, hold hers tightly, listen to her talk, ask her questions. I wanted time to stand still.

Sometimes, as in a dream, time does do our bidding. Expand it to get things accomplished we want, shrink it to bring goodness more quickly. The children in Mississippi lived in a different time warp. Dusty brown feet swinging off the back end of a buggy, they had a different drummer keeping time.

"You've been married before Carol, but you aren't now and why Dalhart? I don't understand that."

"No, I've never been married. I lived with Peter for 5 years, near Sausalito. It was rough sometimes — we seemed cut from different wool, but it was working." She stopped.

"And?"

"He was killed in an airplane crash. It was in the summer, on an Indian reservation in Arizona. He had gone there to help them for two months and was taking off on a hot day with a full load. It was an underpowered Cessna 172 and the plateau was high. He just never got out of ground effect. Hit a little stubby tree, crashed and burned." The memory for her was fresh, painful. I read it across her lips, pursed and hesitant now.

"How did you find out about it?" I asked quietly.

"I was with Pan Am then. Three days after it happened I was in Hong Kong when they told me. As I later learned the details I realized something else. Boarding passengers in Guam I had suddenly become violently ill. I sat in the back and waited for the strange nausea to pass. It made no sense, none at all. It was gone in 15 minutes or so. I felt well enough to serve the breakfast. Peter had crashed at precisely the same time I was boarding that flight. From the accident report and my flight schedule I put the two moments together." There were tears in her eyes and she was waiting for me to rescue her emotions.

I was never comfortable doing that. Sure didn't know the right words. I thought back to the Hanna and sailing beneath the Golden Gate. My friends on the bridge had hidden a piece of paper under my pillow in Zacks West which I didn't discover until much later that night. It said, "Hurry Back, we Love You." It was signed "ALL." It meant more to me than all the brave goodbye hugs the day we departed. I taped it to the bottom of the bunk above me and smiled at it daily for eight and one half months.

I began to tell her about Jim then. How he had said all life was a LOVE story if only we would open to it. "He read my manuscript I have in a folder in my closet at home. I wanted it to be a LOVE story. I haven't been able to finish it. But I'm close. He told me I should share it. But..."

"But what, Rod?" She asked it softly, the tears almost dry in the corners of her marvelous eyes. "... what...?"

I rocked my head forward and looked down at the table. "I don't have all the answers yet." I rolled my head back and let out a deep breath.

With my pen I wrote across one of Pepe's napkins, "Where LOVE is strongest, time is weakest." Turning the paper around, I slid it across the table to her. She silently nodded her head. "It means," I said, "the world is not what it appears, even on a clear day from an open cockpit. But if I wash it over with LOVE, it makes sense to me. My wife, my boys, my dear friends. Bound by a LOVE that just IS, not stuck to the hands of a clock, a season, a lifetime. I look at the thousands of faces in an airport and wonder sometimes how it can be we are One. Then I find just one face at an airport in Dalhart and she shows me again, how LOVE is the reason." Saying it, the words seemed mired still in far off sounds, and syntax. I looked at Carol and knew we both full well understood this thing. We didn't need to speak anymore, except Pepe's patrons might think it odd for two people to be smiling, sitting for hours, few words echoing across the napkin holder. But then I didn't much care about appearances any more.

Pepe's served up a minor feast. Good food in this company seemed entirely correct. We enjoyed the meal while the conversation moved back to easy channels for awhile. I began to believe that if I just opened my mind to the space-time continuum and unfeathered its slowly windmilling prop of limitations, that a solar wind would come to lift the wings of my Fleet and spin the mind's windmill of ideas. Sometimes I felt that all the thoughts ever necessary to gain access to that solar wind had been written and reported, rewritten and restated in every language man had devised. All the religions, all the disciplines, all the antics, the dances and drugs, all were pinioned against the same simple precept — LOVE. Just flip the switch on. And keep it on. Whenever society seemed to want to turn it off, whatever ideas came along to douse it in hate, all I had to do was reach up, in my own personal way, and flip it back on. Not complex, not a soap opera travesty. A simple act, just to LOVE, just to flip that switch "on" every opportunity, every moment. Gandi had said we are the center of a circle without a circumference and Einstein had said we needed to widen the circle of our compassion. I wanted to do that. And that was all I wanted to do. Sitting at a back table in Pepe's on a warm summer night with another world citizen brought to me by forces unseen but expected, I was ready.

Carol had made the clock strike midnight and stop. We left the restaurant to drive the highway back to the Panhandle Inn. As I wheeled the Camaro out on the blacktop she told me it had been a very long time since she had shared her feelings with someone like that. Longer than she cared to remember. She was in Dalhart to drive out the past, away from familiar places and times. It had begun to grow on her, this windy dry landscape. She found tiny niches of fascinating life in the friends here, the free and easy timelessness of its way of dealing with problems. There were a lot of cowboys, "all hat, no cattle" men, but it didn't matter. It was, after all, a piece of the planet like every other. It could be loved. I had dropped from the sky and she had been waiting, just to talk about LOVE and reach out again to a part of the world she left behind.

In particle physics, when two particles interact, change takes place. Energy is transferred, released. Momentum is altered and the colliding particles move off in different directions, no longer the same particles they were before. A physicist could draw a Feynman diagram and tell you mathematically what occurred. When two human beings collide over a Mexican dinner and LOVE is exchanged, they are changed forever and their paths skew off on entirely new directions. But no diagram exists to tell us where it will be... I was tired from the long hours of flying, the wind surging through the cockpit, sun blistering my nose. Tired but aware. This night, a canopy full of stars, the same ones that filled my cockpit over the Gulf, this night was warm, fresh evidence of my convictions grown deep inside, years of effort to draw them out. "Carol, have you ever felt as though you were...have you ever just KNOWN perfectly the size and dimension or your existence, seen it on the point of evolution, encased in a LOVE that was inexpressible? Do you know what I'm trying to say?"

"Yes...I do. It means you LOVE even your enemies. That we are not man and woman in LOVE, we are souls without gender dancing eternally, we are together tonight and we are together forever."

Funny how it happens like that. Years away from the first time I asked the question, first tried so hard to see the answer. Trust it to come and it does. Of its own accord. Life in its most intricate web of flowing design, encircling me with Light.

Time and commitments would cut us off. And perhaps it was best. But there was a glimpse of LOVE and Joy just arrived from Eternity's own mint. We were wealthy and we knew it.

At the Inn, I got out and held open the door for her to slip back into the driver's seat. The west Texas wind gusted through the night, twisting knotted hair before her eyes.

"You'll be needing a ride to the airport in a few hours. What time shall I pick you up?"

"Oh, you don't have to do that. Isn't there a courtesy car here? There must be a cab." Naturally I wanted her to drive me, but I was sliding back to pretenses again.

"Of course not," she smiled, "I'm it."

"You really are. Well, lets see, sunrise is about five thirty, pretty close. Say about five. That ok with you?"

"I'll bring you a biscuit and some orange juice. That should get you to Raton." "Thank you...Carol." I put out my hand to shake hers, feeling awkward and totally inadequate suddenly. I think she knew I wanted to draw her to me and embrace her, hold her for a long moment, this woman who had dropped like a falling star into my midst. I let the wind drown our good nights with Promises to talk some more one day. But that day I knew would be a long way off.

Before I drifted off to sleep, I had the oddest sensation of patterns dancing in my brain, pieces of a puzzle coming together. First there was a Radiant Light friendly and warm. Then a nurse, compassion radiating from her heart. Symbols both, I was certain. Suddenly I saw it. I was sixteen, in the hospital in Missouri. I was age forty, another night, another nurse, and Light filling the darkness in Dalhart. The LOVE they shared was as strong and mysterious as anything I had known. Just one thing was missing. I closed my eyes but then I thought of Mick Cael, now a pilot with Republic - saw him laughing somewhere on the planet, a cigar jammed in the middle of his mouth — saw him asking, "where you been, Maggot?" I chuckled. Mick, if you only knew! I slept soundly till the phone rang at four thirty. It was Carol. Time to wake up. She would be here in half an hour. I rubbed the sleep from my eyes, wished them a good morning and promised them a day full of adventure. It was always wonderful to wake up to go flying like this. Strange sheets and far away places and in the middle of all that, a sweet Texas voice saying "Good morning."

I splashed water on my beard and got the process under way — a shave and a quick shower.

The biscuits were wrapped in hot tin foil, already buttered. Some jam was in a jar on the dashboard, beside the orange juice. I finished it all on the ride to the airport. Carol looked fresh and happy, wearing her Levi's again and new sneakers.

I preflighted the Fleet, stowed my baggage and had Carol handle the throttle. The Kinner's eight foot wooden prop looks imposing up close. It had almost knocked my hand off once, but it was friendly enough, if you respected it. With gas dripping out the carburetor, a little tug past the click of the magnetos and she caught, fired right off in the early morning silence. The old engines don't roar so much as click, like the inside of a factory full of weaving looms. She needed time to warm up too.

Carol had that wistful look that told me she wished she were coming along. Every romantic in the world would have chosen this morning to fly. The sun just below the eastern horizon, sending shafts of light to pierce the retreating night. No wind. Two quiet souls standing beside one another and a red and yellow Fleet. I saw it from a distance, another old movie, but one I had selected. Engine warming, smelling like warm grease and castor oil. The Fleet was patient. Had been here many times before. I knew that. Knew it sure as I knew anything... Lord, this was perfection.

I zipped my scruffy leather jacket up and tucked the scarf in the space where the little "v" of an opening would be a pipeline for the morning's cool air unless I blocked it. The sun would warm the back of my neck as I flew, plus a little of my right cheek. I could count on it as I warmed in the cockpit a thousand feet above Texas and New Mexico.

"Thank you." I spoke just a little above the clapping of the engine "Carol" I said, "I wish you were flying with me this morning. Got any relatives or friends in Oregon you need to visit?"

"This is your adventure. What waits over the horizon is fresh, waiting for you, without extra baggage. But I would love to go...another time." There was nothing left to say now. The Fleet was ready, probably anxious. A time machine vibrates in harmony with the Universe, no waiting for two conscious souls slowly agreeing to meet again in other futures. I climbed into the rear cockpit, settling myself as comfortably as I could, readying the sectional chart, folded just right for the leg to Raton. There is a moment or two that a cockpit feels awkward when I first slide into it. The rudder pedals need adjustment, or the back of the seat is pushing in a soft spot where it hasn't before. This tiny bridge of time is all that is necessary before my body disappears among the longerons and cables and flows secretly to the wingtips. Words that wrestle with the prop blast become lip synched and cliche. I snapped my summer green fabric helmet in place, the goggles set high on my forehead. Carol reached in and gently lifted the shoulder straps so I could buckle them. Our quiet smiles met for an instant, close enough to feel her breath warm my neck.

I reached up with a hand and put two fingers to my lips. In Navy formation flying, the signal to break up was to motion with the fingers, making a sign like "kissing off." I thought of it as I held my fingers on my lips a moment, then made the old Navy sign. She stepped back, smiled and blew a kiss that found its way through the tidal wave of air swirling around me as I jazzed the throttle, holding the brakes and the stick back. I shouted through a cupped hand another "Thank you, Carol," as I released the brakes and taxied forward before kicking the rudder to move out towards the waiting runway.

My concentration returned to the cockpit: gauges, charts, trim, loose scarf, helmet buttoned, goggles strap snapped on the helmet. There was no gray sea surrounding me, no green Mark 82's strapped to the underside of my wings, no frantic flight deck crews running in race track patterns. The sun was sifting through the sagebrush, two red wing blackbirds taking flight across the taxiway as I neared them.

How peaceful I thought. How incredibly beautiful this poem of morning, written before I ever was, that will ever be, long after I am. Alone with this aircraft—turned—magic carpet, rolling to the take off end of a runway pointed in every direction I would ever choose: to fly this morning would be to wake up alive, truly alive. I spun the Fleet around and ran up the Kinner, checking the magnetos left and right, the stick and rudders free to travel.

At the far end, beside the gas shack, Carol waited. For her the Fleet was a slowly coloring silhouette of wing over wing, struts and wires backlit by the sunrise. The emerging clatter of the Kinner came a moment after the takeoff roll began. She walked three steps out from the shack and watched.

To takeoff in the Fleet, I merely think about it. Ease the throttle back after liftoff to baby the engine, climb slowly and watch the earth give way. Sometimes it seems life begins, for me, at the takeoff end of a runway. Perhaps it's untrue, but I want to believe it drifting across the country in my cockpit open to leaves and stardust and dripping cloud. Wishing it to be must make it so. And there, arms raised in slow circles of goodbye, Carol grows, a wildflower that blooms in the Texas night. I pull my left hand from the throttle and out of the cockpit, waving in slow, exaggerated motions. The Fleet is headed toward Raton and a day of no boredom under her wings. I share a last brief smile with Carol and move the wings left—right left—right, wagging across the Dalhart morning sky. She is down there, I am here in this drafty cocoon, caterpillar changing to butterfly. How different it is, I think, to touch a soul as I did last night than it is to unleash TNT in their life. I don't want to dream anymore and not DO. Not DO the things I dream and know are right for me. This morning is right. It's right for the Universe. But I am a single cell on a voyage of discovery, me and my loving carried like a seed to high desert places. Somehow I want to grow up everywhere, to know that times like this will never go away, will be waiting there in the wings for anyone willing to ask for and believe in them.

I glance at my watch, then the grain elevators of Dalhart, standing naked in the early sun, sweet smelling flagships of the desert. Roll on, I prayed, through my watch, through the Integrity Watch of the years. Guarding grain, every seed mirroring life. Why is it we do not feed the starving everywhere on the planet? Economics in college never gave me a satisfactory answer, only excuses. With enough Fleets, with excess 707's and DC-8's baking in the Arizona deserts, surely enough LOVE and energy exists to do it. From five hundred feet over Dalhart, summer, five forty in the morning, no excuses hold up. I know a truth that cannot be dismantled with economics.

With the sun warming my neck now half an hour out of Dalhart I ponder something which has hovered like a ghost around my thinking. Carol Martin WAS that Radiant Person I waited for, had met in my dream during the island storm. Come and gone but still a presence. And I began to smile again as I realized that Carol had known my destination was Oregon BEFORE I told her. I looked back over my shoulder towards Dalhart and shouted, "Carol!" I knew she heard me, knew she was no longer there, had been there JUST for me. That people slip into our lives to give us LOVE and Answers and then are gone, flying on the wind that circles the planet.

"Whew!" I said, running my gaze from horizon to horizon ahead of me. I fixed my eyes on the cork in the gas gauge that was still comfortably high. With enough 80 octane and rocker arm grease, I could circle the planet, meet all the Radiant People with LOVE and Answers that I would ever need. And I laughed out loud, shouting it to the wind racing past my cockpit.

I thought of all those Radiant People who were part of my life. Alison and the boys, my close friends. All had that special Radiance if I looked closely. And where are you this morning Case? Hiding under Commander's gold bars in the Pentagon. And Oink? I looked overhead for a Southwest airliner. Where are you today Captain Brunson? I kicked the nose of the Fleet to one side a little and looked back towards the hidden elevators marking Dahlhart. "We are all precious" she had said last night: "each of us a giving—taking—loving, connected part of the Universe. Share LOVE. Express it with enthusiasm."

"YES!" I whistled as I rocked the Fleet up into a steep bank back on course. Following highway 87 now, where there are only one or two semi's wheeling west, fewer headed east. I see the approaching Kiowa grasslands. The land is rising above five thousand feet but the Fleet is not objecting in the cool air. I slip past the tractor trailers slowly, creeping toward Raton pulled by the giant wooden windmill in front of me. The sky is clear in every quadrant. The world below sleeps a last few winks, hears the tapping of a new day on its windowsill; work to be done, things to be learned.

There is a bright yellow school bus ahead, and I drop down to fly beside it. The windows fill with eyes and pointing fingers and smiles. They are racing down highway 87 towards Clayton, country kids on their way to something, a summer retreat perhaps. I am here to peer across the space that separates us to be reminded that none really does. The Fleet glints in the sunlight, a thing of joy to behold — I see me in the bus, once a child filled with dreams of flying - so happy now this future me is moving the stick, tapping the rudders, smiling through the past and present. Here you are dear children of the summer, a pirouette of freedom for you, a memory cast in sunshine and LOVE. The Fleet sweeps up and away and I thought then of evolution and eternity. We are marching through time, passengers on a flight into the Unknown. But we know it. Know now that we will evolve forever. We, the first generation to have the ability to obliterate life, to push itself into extinction, never will. The solemn futures of generations past had world wars written among their choices. This one does not. How bright and promising to know they are behind us. That wars will fade into antiquity, rapidly, as the creature called society discovers its whole body and its home are One. That only four letters, just two words describe all that is necessary for us to remember — LOVE and Evolve.

It would be easy to forget it all if the engine quit right now, I thought. But that wouldn't change it. My family would know I loved them no matter what. Friends from the Hanna and squadron mates would not object if we found LOVE to be the force unfolding creation.

The grasslands spread in waves to the boundless horizon. Wave upon wave in the wind, weaving patterns across an emerald sea. My dreams would come and go but their effect would not... I tapped the control stick with my finger. There was no trigger on it, no bomb pickle button. Only an old bicycle grip met my hand. I could never leave my past, but my present was better and the futures were in the shape of true joysticks ~ no weapons hinged to them. I was keeping the switch "on"- the LOVE which formed the boundary layer over my wings; the LOVE which drew light reflected from the earth into my eyes; the LOVE that drew me once to war to learn its perfect lesson. I let the guilt fly on, released the old pain, unhooked the tether I had dragged behind -- let it go with LOVE -- a tiny helium balloon free to travel the biosphere. In the cockpit of the Fleet this bright summer morning, once again the world made sense.

EPILOGUE 1984

Where are they now, my old squadron mates and friends?

Turkey is a Commander, working in Washington, not flying. Turkey and the Maid of Cotton have three little gobblers.

Oink is a Captain with Southwest Airlines. Mick flies for Republic Airlines. They are both still single. Bear Smith became a Blue Angel. Flies DC—9's now.

Tracey, to whom I wrote a sheaf of letters, married an Air Force pilot but later divorced. She is remarried now and living in the Sunshine State.

Bev got pregnant when Mike Norwood came home. Before the baby came, Mike, inexplicably, spun in and died in his jet in the Gulf of Mexico off Pensacola.

Most of us are still around, somewhere, dancing through life each day as it arrives. Life goes on whether there is a war or not. Goes on for those that survived that is.

I never really talked with any of my friends about what it felt like to KILL other human beings. We were so caught up in just trying to survive it seemed useless to ask that kind of question. But I don't think they much cared for the work either. They may have other reasons and ideas and maybe they don't think much about it anymore. That's ok too because its past now. But I'd like to sit down and kick it around today, see what kind of dreams they have now, hear what they plan to do to keep evolving.

Perhaps I am a lonely single cell of humanity who is weary of war, big bombs, silver bullets, terrorists, and innocent deaths. And this was just another father's wish for his children to find better ways to get along with enemy-friends. If I believed that though, I think I would have tucked this all away in a manila folder for just Scott and Ryan to read someday.

YELLOW STICKY NOTE:
EPILOGUE 2015

My whimsical Aerosculptures include the elements of cloud, wind, water, "G" water, music and folklore in a delicate, yet powerful, ephemeral performance which disappears as it is created yet is never forgotten."

Rod Magner, Orcas Island Artists Registry, 2000

Thirty years since I wrote the manuscript...time flies and so should you! Now, 2015, I will finish the 25th year flying my 1929 TravelAir biplane. Seven thousand plus hours, 10,000 landings on Orcas Island, 20,000 passengers, two at a time. I have been an aerial Noah's Ark and, critically, master of my own identity, my own destiny. I have a tiny white biplane sticker on my rear window, my symbol for I LOVE (being the master of my destiny). I have now a whole new story, written across my digital heaven, here on one of the most re-markable joys on the planet, Orcas Island. I have watched, I have trusted, I have learned. This story is in another manuscript. Waiting patiently for its morning Light.

This book had to come first. But since you asked me Mick so long ago, Where You Been Boy? has had ever changing answers.

LOVE has only one.

Stop by my hangar sometime during the summers where the sign reads:

WELCOME
We Listen to your Stories

Small Lies, Simple Joys, Occasional Truths

You are of course welcome to visit anytime these sites below:
magicair.com :my business on Orcas Island

And now, in 2016, retired.

littlemagic.com   : my next business

GLOSSARY

A4 = designation for the Skyhawk, a single seat jet

A7 = designation for a single seat jet, newer, more advanced systems than the A4

20 MIKE MIKE = 20 millimeter shells fired by guns on A4

37mm = number used to describe size of shells fired from anti-aircraft guns

AILERON = control device on wings used to roll aircraft

ANGELS = altitude

ANGLE OF ATTACK = the angle the wing is meeting the air

APPROACH = the route flown to a landing; or the people on the ground radar guiding the aircraft

BDA = bomb damage assessment

BALL = an orange colored light on the ground or ship used to aid landings

BARCAP = BARrier CArrier Patrol, flown by fighters to protect carrier

BIRD FARM = slang among carrier pilots for a "carrier"

BREAK = a point beside the runway or just ahead of the carrier where each aircraft peels off from formation and slows for landing

CAG = Commander of the Air Wing; which is all the various squadrons deployed aboard a carrier

CATWALK = a walkway just below the flight deck level attached to some outside sections of the ship

COD = carrier—on—board—delivery; the aircraft that flies mail and passengers out to the carrier

CSD = constant speed drive; a device attached to the engine which produces the aircraft electricity

CYCLE = period of time between launch and recovery of planes

DMZ = demilitarized zone

EAGLES = radio call sign of VA—212 flying A4's

F8 = the fabulous Chance Vought jet fighter aircraft, single piloted, last of the gun fighters

FAC = forward air controller

FEET WET = code for flying "over water"

FLEET = biplane

FOX CORPEN = the heading of the ship

FUEL STATE = the amount of fuel remaining in the tanks, sometimes shortened to "state"

GARFISH = radio call sign for VA—55, an A4 squadron

GUARD = an emergency radio frequency monitored by ground and air rescue stations and vehicles

GUN TUB = the area on side of carrier where large guns were mounted

KBA = people "killed by air" delivered weapons

KINNER = name of engine used on Fleet biplane

LINE PERIOD = time the carrier is at sea, engaged in combat

LOVE = item forgotten and trampled in wars

LSO = landing signal officer; the man standing beside the landing area on the carrier monitoring the approach of each aircraft

MAGIC STONE = radio call sign of VA-164, my squadron

MARK 32 = a 500 pound bomb

MAX ENDURANCE = aircraft being flown throttled back to conserve fuel

NAIL 5-3 = radio call sign of FAC aircraft spotting targets

NATOPS official book on aircraft describing all its systems

0 CLUB = officers club

PBY = old, heavy, slow navy amphibian aircraft, piston engined

PLAT = pilots landing aid television; a tv monitor in every ready room where landings are replayed for grading

POL = petroleum; used in damage reports to describe petroleum drums hit

PRC 90 = small hand held walkie talkie radio used for emergencies

PICKLE = to drop your bombs. Button on stick pressed to release them

PIDGEONS = the distance and heading to some point

PIPPER = a tiny pink lighted "v" in the center of the gunsight

146

PIRAZ = name of the ship used to detect enemy aircraft

PLANE GUARD = the ship that follows the carrier for rescues

PROBE = on the A4 a long pipe with a nozzle at its tip used to aerial refuel

RAT = ram air turbine; an emergency electrical generator deployed into the airstream

READY ROOM = the squadron's headquarters aboard the carrier

ROCKET NUMBER = the lineal number of each pilot according to rank in the squadron

SORTIE = one mission flown by one aircraft T-28 = old Navy piston engined trainer with 1425 horsepower radial engine

SKIPPER = CO =Commanding Officer of a squadron or ship

SPEED BRAKES= two large panels under the horizontal tail that deploy outward to help slow you

TALLY HO = slang for "I have you in sight"

TANKER = aircraft equipped to transfer fuel in the air to others; the A4 could be so configured

TRAP = slang for an arrested landing aboard a carrier

WINCHESTER = term used to indicate you have no ordnance left

www.ingramcontent.com/pod-product-compliance
Lightning Source LLC
Chambersburg PA
CBHW071542040426
42452CB00008B/1085